# TRACE YOUR FAMILY TREE

## FAMILY MATTERS ✓

# TRACING YOUR FAMILY TREE

**SEAN CALLERY**

WARD LOCK

First published in Great Britain in 1991
by Ward Lock Limited, Villiers House,
41/47 Strand, London WC2N 5JE, England

A Cassell Imprint

© Ward Lock Limited 1991

All rights reserved. No part of this publication
may be reproduced or transmitted in any form
or by any means, electronic or mechanical
including photocopying, recording or
any information storage or retrieval system,
without prior permission in writing from
the publishers.

**British Library Cataloguing in Publication Data**

Callery, Sean
  Tracing Your Family Tree – (Family matters)
  1. Family trees
  I. Title   II. Series
  929.1

  ISBN 0–7063–6947–5

Typeset in 11 on 11½ point ITC Garamond Light by
Columns Design and Production
Services Ltd, Reading

Printed and bound in Great Britain by
William Collins & Sons, Glasgow

# CONTENTS

| | | |
|---|---|---|
| **INTRODUCTION** | | 7 |
| **Chapter 1:** | **THE WAY AHEAD** | 9 |
| **Chapter 2:** | **KEEPING TRACK** | 14 |
| **Chapter 3:** | **INTERVIEWING RELATIVES** | 24 |
| **Chapter 4:** | **CIVIL RECORDS** | 33 |
| **Chapter 5:** | **PARISH RECORDS** | 42 |
| **Chapter 6:** | **WILLS** | 58 |
| **Chapter 7:** | **NEWSPAPERS** | 62 |
| **Chapter 8:** | **SERVICE AND PROFESSIONAL RECORDS** | 64 |
| **Chapter 9:** | **MAPS AND LAND RECORDS** | 68 |
| **Chapter 10:** | **IMMIGRATION AND EMIGRATION** | 73 |
| **Chapter 11:** | **THE ORIGINS OF NAMES** | 77 |
| **Chapter 12:** | **HERALDRY** | 83 |
| **Chapter 13:** | **WRITING UP YOUR FAMILY HISTORY** | 88 |
| **SOME USEFUL ADDRESSES** | | 91 |
| **INDEX** | | 95 |

# INTRODUCTION
# TRACING YOUR FAMILY TREE

Most of us know quite a lot about our parents, and something about our grandparents. It is knowledge acquired through the experience of being with them when we were young. As we grow older we enjoy finding out more about, say, how they earned a living, when they married, and where they lived. These are all scraps of information that help to give us a greater insight into our past. Putting together the pieces of the jigsaw is great fun and adds to our sense of who we are.

However, our knowledge of our ancestors usually stops a short way down the line. Go back more than two or three generations, and you probably know very little. What will you find through your detective work? A roving sailor? A local mayor? An aristocrat with blue blood? Perhaps you will discover a new branch of your own family through a long-lost relative. Provided you can trace your relatives the chances are you will find a wide variety of characters, because every person you identify was brought into the world by two more people — the sheer numbers involved as you travel through the generations are amazing! Go back three generations to your great great grandparents and your family tree will contain at least 31 names, with a further 32 waiting the next stage back.

We all have so many past relatives that there is bound

## INTRODUCTION

to be a social mix — look at the 64 great great great grandparents of the Queen Mother: they include two dukes, daughters of a duke and a marquess, three earls and one earl's daughter, a viscount, a baron, six country gentlemen, a director of the East India Company, a banker, two bishop's daughters, three clergymen, the daughter of a Huguenot refugee, an Irish officer, an inn landlord, and a plumber and toymaker from London. This strange mixture of past relatives also explains why you may have a family coat of arms. Although these were generally only allowed to the nobility, family fortunes, like investments on the Stock Exchange, can go up as well as down. Indeed, one of the thrills of genealogy is to watch the soap opera of rising and falling fortunes of your family over the years.

This book provides guidance on how to set about the task of tracing your family tree. However, because every family is different, there are no precise step-by-step rules for this; for example, while one person may go from interviewing relatives to checking marriage certificates, someone else may not have many relatives still alive and will need to work from birth certificates.

The best way to use this book is to read it through once to get an idea of the various avenues of research and how to go about them. Then go back to the beginning and start putting the pieces together and see where the clues are taking you. It is a safe bet that once you start looking into your ancestry, you won't want to stop — and your researches will take you on strange and unexpected paths. I hope you enjoy the journey!

# Chapter 1

# THE WAY AHEAD

Tracing your family tree may, at first, seem a daunting prospect. But in fact you will follow through a series of quite simple moves, made at whatever pace you choose. When you put together the information revealed by each move, you can begin to assemble the jigsaw of who your ancestors are.

You should start by finding out as much as you can from living relatives, then check the information they supply. After this, you can begin tracking down the next generation back from the stage you have reached (probably your grandparents). Like all family detectives you will have a choice of which line of heritage to follow. Most genealogists start by following the male line, from father to father. Some may try to concentrate on the female line (mother to mother), but this is hard to trace as women usually change their names on marriage. The important thing is to set a target, such as 'Go back five generations on my father's side' and when you have met it, decide whether to continue following this trail or start another.

Your researches will include a number of activities, from getting copies of documents to tracing immigration records. The following 20 steps will give you some idea of what you will be doing, in roughly the order listed (although this will vary with every family tree).

**Step 1:** Set up your filing system so that you have good records of where you have searched and

## THE WAY AHEAD

what you have found out — and how you can find it again!

**Step 2:** Interview as many relatives as you can, gathering information, photographs and family documents.

**Step 3:** Take time and examine all such documents carefully.

**Step 4:** Check all data on names, birth and marriage dates of grandparents by **obtaining copies of certificates from St Catherine's House** (or other sources if outside England and Wales — see useful addresses at the end of this book).

**Step 5:** Start drawing up your family tree in rough form so that it can be amended and updated.

**Step 6:** Get more detail on the ancestors, particularly grandparents, you have identified. For male ancestors, you should probably try military records as they are likely to have been involved in one of the two World Wars. Perhaps someone moved abroad; the Public Record Office at Kew lists **passport applications from 1795 onwards**.

**Step 7:** Using the copies of your grandparents' birth and marriage certificates, trace their parents via the **civil records** (birth and marriage certificates) **which go back to 1837** (1855 for Scotland).

**Step 8:** Update your family tree chart with all the information you have gathered so far. You are probably **back into the second half of the nineteenth century** by now.

**Step 9:** Using civil records such as birth certificates, go on to gather more dates through **the Census Returns from 1881 backwards**. These will supply you with birth dates and occupation details. Census Returns are a valuable source of detail for the family detective.

## THE WAY AHEAD

**Step 10:** You will now need to move on to **check parish records which can take you back to 1753 or earlier** in the locality that your ancestors inhabited to get information on births and marriages. For this you may need to contact a County Record Office, or perhaps the International Genealogical Index (IGI) or Percival Boyd Index (**which covers 1538–1837**).

**Step 11:** Once you establish where and when ancestors died, get copies of local newspapers and try to find an obituary.

**Step 12:** If you know in which graveyard an ancestor was buried, visit the cemetery and examine any inscription on the gravestone.

**Step 13:** Check any ancestral **wills at the Principal Probate Registry or Scottish Record Office**. These go back to 1858 and may include mentions of other relatives. Also try the Prerogative Court of Canterbury which has **an index of wills from 1383–1700**.

**Step 14:** Look for references to ancestors in the sixteenth century Poor Law and land ownership and tenancy records from the County Record Office.

**Step 15:** Update your family chart again, and marvel at how much progress you have made.

**Step 16:** Continue the process of finding each new generation and checking their details. You may take a particular interest in a person or a trade in which your ancestors were involved, so your research may be diverted for a while as you follow this up.

**Step 17:** You are quite likely to find the trail goes cold. Start to check for records of ancestors in adjacent parishes — they may well have moved away, but the chances are they did not travel far.

**Step 18:** Start looking into the origins of your family name — you may be close to finding the first person to carry it!

**Step 19:** Read some of the local or national newspapers of the time of an ancestor who particularly interests you. This will give you more idea of what everyday life was like for him or her.

**Step 20:** Keep going! If you are very lucky, you may eventually end up at the **Domesday Book which dates from 1086**!

## CLUES TO LOOK OUT FOR

1. A family crest or coat of arms on any official family documents or seals.
2. An ancestor who was involved in some famous event, battle or who shares a name with a well-known person from that era. You may choose to widen your research at this point to find out more about them.
3. New ancestors you did not expect to find — perhaps a half-brother of a relative of yours. You may find a whole new avenue of research opens up!
4. Famous ancestors. They may have been written about in a biography or history of their time.
5. Odd-looking names. These may indicate a new strand of ancestors, perhaps immigrants.
6. Ancestors with non-conformist (usually Catholic or Jewish) backgrounds: these will take you on a new path of discovery.

## SOURCES CHECKLIST

The chief sources of basic information are as follows. Most can be contacted by post if you do not want to make a personal visit.

## SOURCES CHECKLIST

1. Living relatives.
2. Civil records. (Official documents like birth certificates, held at Register Offices).
3. Parish records (usually at County Record Offices, and many also stored in the International Genealogical Index).
4. Census Returns (held in the Public Record Office).
5. Wills (stored at the Principal Probate Registry or Scottish Record Office).
6. Other documents, from newspapers to military or manorial records.

Whichever direction you choose to go in, you must first check if anyone else has traced all or part of your family tree already. It is surprisingly common for people to spend perhaps many years delving into their ancestry — and then find that they are following in the steps of a past relative who may have got further. Even if you find you only go back a couple of centuries in your research, you have created a family heirloom that someone else can keep going. However much or little you do, you will find the rewards enormous.

# Chapter 2

# KEEPING TRACK

Tracing the family tree is so fascinating it may become an obsession, but it requires careful organisation and hard work. The task of dredging up and checking information is formidable enough, but making sense of it, and keeping it in a form which allows you to roam through it searching for a particular reference is a demanding job in itself.

## CHECKLIST OF EARLY AIMS

Your targets as you start your researches are:

1. Set up a filing system which is logically structured and easily understood.
2. Begin a rough chart of the family tree, to be added to throughout your researches and neatly reproduced when you are happy with them.
3. Keep a thorough record of what you have researched, what is planned for research, and where documents are stored.

## FILING SYSTEM

It is best to start by setting up your information storage system so that as you become engrossed in the business of gathering facts you can file them efficiently.

## FILING SYSTEM

If you have a personal computer, you will know that computer discs are capable of holding many thousands of pieces of information, and you are probably familiar with the best filing pattern provided through your software. One point to be made here is that you must regularly copy your discs, so that you always have at least two copies of everything you have discovered. Too many people learn the importance of making copies the hard way — when they lose a disc.

Even if you do have a personal computer, you will probably find it easier to use a manual filing system, at least initially. One of the best manual filing systems for the family detective involves the use of a card index in which each person is recorded on an individual card.

For easy access to information it is best to use a different coloured card for each side of the family. So you may write details of the male line (from your father through his parents and so on) on blue cards, with details of the female line (from your mother's parents) stored on red cards. You may choose to use the same colour cards throughout but mark them with different coloured marker pens to make these distinctions.

Each card should contain the following information:

1. Surname and first name(s)
2. Date of birth
3. Place of birth
4. Date of marriage(s)
5. Place of marriage(s)
6. Father's name
7. Mother's maiden name
8. Spouse's name
9. Names and sex of children

Also on the front of the card there should be some details about the person, together with references to where notes or documents about them are kept. Keep these notes in plastic folders in numbered or colour-coded box files. At the front of each box there should be a full list of contents, which you must add to with each additional document. You will be surprised how many pieces of paper you gather through your researches, and by being painstaking about keeping a record of where everything is, you are saving yourself hours of worried searching through untidy piles of papers later on!

The card should also carry a reference number because you are going to need to cross-index various pieces of information as you build up the tree. As you start each colour card, simply begin by numbering each one in turn from 1 upwards. You will use the colours of the cards to form the full reference number, by adding the initial letter of each colour (B for blue, R for red, etc). So your references to cards relating to the male line will be R1, R2, R3 and so on. This will make them easy to locate when you are checking for a source, correct spelling of a first name, or whatever. If you want to start a card for someone but you are not sure what side of the family they should come under, use a white card and transfer the information to the correct colour card later.

The cards can then be stored in alphabetical order in a suitable container such as a plastic box or an old shoe box. It does not really matter provided the contents are not likely to get re-shuffled if the box is moved, and that there is a lid to keep dust out. You may decide to separate different parts of the family into smaller groups. If you do, use a larger size card as a barrier between each group to keep them separate.

With this system you will be able to pull out details on any person you have come across in your research, together with a source for background information if required. You will also avoid later confusion over the identity, say, of two people in the family with the same name (this is very common as children are often named after a relative or ancestor).

# FAMILY TREE CHART

You will also need either a card index or an address book noting names and addresses of everyone you speak to and of useful contacts or organisations. Record offices, bookshops, relatives... the list will grow with your researches, and you will find a directory of this information will save a lot of time. Some useful addresses are listed at the end of this book. Whatever the system, update it regularly and keep it flexible: as facts are verified or fail to be authenticated, the overall picture and your specific aims may change.

## FAMILY TREE CHART

You will most likely want to maintain an updating chart showing your progress to date. Even starting one now will give you some sense of satisfaction as once you get to great grandparents you can easily fill a sheet of paper with the relevant names and dates!

Because much of the information you gather, particularly at first, will be from people's memories — which are notoriously unreliable for supplying accurate dates — you should treat your early research as provisional. You may wish to enter such details in pencil, to be inked in if, and when, the facts are confirmed.

The chart can look quite rough at the beginning, because it will be amended and added to quite a lot over the course of your research. Start with a large piece of paper, with your name and date of birth at the top in the centre, then draw a short vertical line and then a longer horizontal line. Write your mother's name on the left end of it, and your father's on the right, with an = sign between them and the date of the marriage (= is the usual symbol for a marriage). Then repeat the process using their parents' names. You will end up with a chart looking like the one on page 18.

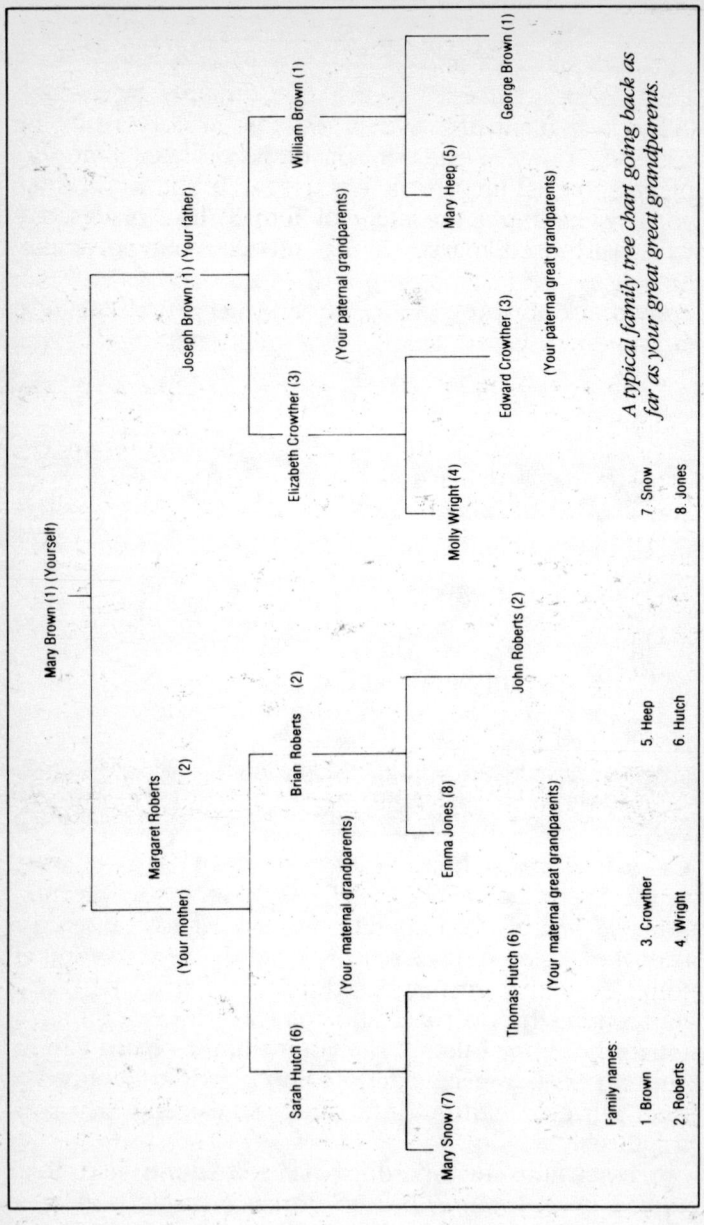

You may choose to buy a blank family tree chart and simply fill in the names. Do this in pencil first in case you make a mistake or find out later that the information is incorrect. When you fill it in in ink, you may highlight the male or female line of descent with a coloured marker if this reflects your particular interest.

Try to follow these guidelines to keep your chart neat and understandable:

1. Keep people of the same generation level with one another.
2. Draw the line of descent of children from underneath the = marriage symbol.
3. If a man married twice, put the first wife (labelled [1]) on the left, the second (labelled [2]) on the right; vice versa for a woman who married twice.
4. Record children in order of birth whenever possible.
5. Do not allow the lines of descent (pedigree lines) to overlap.

# RECORD YOUR RESEARCH

It is as important to record your sources as it is your findings, so that you can prove the validity of information you gather. You should also note down all other areas of research undertaken, even if they produced nothing, so that you or anyone following up on your work does not cover the same ground twice. There are few things more frustrating than making a return trip to view a parish register, and realising you have already been through it thoroughly and your second visit was pointless!

A source listing should read something like this: *Copied by Peter Small from Parish Register, Northolt.*

# KEEPING TRACK

*Baptisms 1860–1912. All CARRUTHERS entries checked, 3/1/91.* That means that Peter Small examined all entries relating to the CARRUTHERS surname covering the period 1860–1912 in the Northolt Parish Register, on 3 January 1991, and copied out the relevant references.

As you can see the surname here is written in CAPITALS. This is standard practice in genealogy as it helps to make lists of names easier to read and understand. Whenever you are writing up your notes, you must feel confident that you would be able to make sense of them if you had to re-read them in two years' time. If you can't, you are wasting effort.

---

## ROMAN NUMERALS CHECKLIST

Whatever documents you are examining, you are very likely to come across the use of Roman numerals, especially for dates. This can be confusing if you are not familiar with reading such figures. The following guide will help.

| | | | |
|---|---|---|---|
| I = 1 | XI = 11 | XXX = 30 | CCCC or CD = 400 |
| II = 2 | XII = 12 | XL = 40 | D = 500 |
| III = 3 | XIII = 13 | L = 50 | DC = 60 |
| IV = 4 | XIV = 14 | LX = 60 | DCC = 700 |
| V = 5 | XV = 15 | LXX = 70 | DCCC = 800 |
| VI = 6 | XVI = 16 | LXXX = 80 | CM = 900 |
| VII = 7 | XVII = 17 | XC = 90 | M = 1000 |
| VIII = 8 | XVIII = 18 | C = 100 | MM = 2000 |
| IX = 9 | XIX = 19 | CC = 200 | |
| X = 10 | XX = 20 | CCC = 300 | |

Numbers may also appear in Latin. One to ten are as follows: Unus, duo, tres, quattuor, quninque, sex, septem, octo, novem, decem.

## STORING DOCUMENTS

You will gather a number of documents, such as photocopies of birth certificates, photographs, and other papers which you will want to be able to refer to but maintain in good condition. If they are just thrown into a box file they will get creased, folded and torn — besides becoming rather well-thumbed as you flick past looking for another document.

The answer is to use a file with clear plastic pockets — most good stationers sell them — then each document can be kept separate, easy to examine, and free of dust. Two can be placed back to back in each pocket. Stickers on each folder should identify the documents and carry a reference number. Record each addition to your file on a sheet of paper stored on the inner sleeve, giving its date and number. This file will be very useful for you both in proving sources of information if there are queries, and when you come to write up the family history (see Chapter 13).

---

### RESEARCH CHECKLIST

1. Record the information you gather straightaway.
2. Don't skip to save time, or to avoid things you would rather not know. Quite a few families have a skeleton in the cupboard of some kind, and you may chance upon it!
3. Note down the source of all information, and the date it was gathered.
4. Keep a thorough research record, of where you went or wrote and when.
5. Record failures as well as successes — they can prove valuable in the end.

## CHECKLIST OF WHAT TO TAKE ON RESEARCH TRIPS

1. Lots of pencils. Some organisations won't allow the use of pens at all.
2. Plenty of paper — a notebook is best.
3. An eraser.
4. Pencil sharpener.
5. A magnifying glass (sometimes you have to peer pretty closely to decipher a handwritten or badly reproduced document).
6. Small change to pay for copying of documents.

## COMMON ABBREVIATIONS

Because of the large amount of information squeezed into a small space, abbreviations flourish in the documents viewed and produced by genealogists. You are likely to come across, and may want to use, the following:

=   married
**Admon.**   Letters of Administration
**b. or brn.**   born
**bach.**   bachelor
**bapt.**   baptised
**bns.**   banns
**b.o.t.p.**   both of this parish
**bur.**   buried
**Cod.**   Codicil
**Ct.**   Court
**d.**   died
**dat.**   dated
**dau.**   daughter
**div.**   divorced
**d.s.p.**   died childless
**d. unm.**   died unmarried
**educ.**   educated at
**eld.**   eldest

**STORING DOCUMENTS**

**f.** female or father — the context will indicate which
**g.f.** grandfather
**g.g.f.** great grandfather
**h.** heir
**inf.** infant
**inv.** inventory
**jnr.** junior
**Lic.** licence
**liv.** living (for example if you know the person was still alive in 1733, liv. 1733)
**m. or marr.** married
**M.I.** Monumental Inscription (wording on a tombstone)
**o.t.p.** of this parish
**P.R.** Parish Register
**P.C.C.** Prerogative Court of Canterbury
**P.C.Y.** Prerogative Court of York
**P.R.O.** Public Record Office
**s.** son
**temp.** time of (as in, time of Elizabeth I)
**unm.** unmarried
**wid.** widow
**wdr.** widower
**w.** wife
**Will pr.** Will proved

# Chapter 3

# INTERVIEWING RELATIVES

The first step toward tracing your family tree is to talk to as many members of your known family as you can. This requires more work than you may think, as you need to prepare carefully for the interview — you want to make it interesting for the other person, while obtaining and retaining as much accurate information as possible.

In the case of older relatives, it could be the only opportunity you have to speak with them, and you do not want them to feel harassed — but you would like them to tell you all they know about the family. They are likely to find the experience highly enjoyable as they recollect incidents perhaps for the first time in years, and your interest will flatter them.

If you think you have relatives living in a certain town or area, but do not have any contact with them, try placing an advertisement in the personal column of the local newspaper. Head the advertisement with your family name in bold type — few people are able to resist such an intriguing bait. Explain briefly that you are researching into this family's ancestry and where you can be contacted. It should read something like this:

### **HEADLEY**

I am tracing the Headley family tree, and would like to talk with anyone who bears the Headley name, or has done in the past. Complete confidentiality given if required. Please contact me at (address).

Once you meet your relative, the interview need not be a formal event, but it is worth preparing for it so that you get as much as possible out of it, and do not waste other people's time. Fortunately you can practise this, as you should start by interviewing your spouse, then both sets of parents, who you are likely to know fairly well anyway! The reason you should start in this way is that it helps you to identify all relatives and likely sources of information. You may have an uncle or step grandmother nobody has mentioned to you before.

Your research into the family tree may prompt close relatives to reveal their existence, because they know that eventually you may find them anyway. So by starting at the most obvious places, you can save a lot of time. You should aim to speak to every known relative. Skipping one increases the risk of missing out a vital link in the chain. Clearly a lot of time has to be allocated to this task so be patient and enjoy the contact you have with all these people whom you might never have met. Because of the expense of travelling, you may have to do some interviews by phone.

## INTERVIEW GUIDANCE

1. Contact the relative in advance, and make an appointment to see them or phone them when they have sufficient time for the interview. You are likely to need at least an hour. By forewarning them of the interview, you are allowing them time to gather their thoughts and retrieve any useful papers, photographs or other relevant reminders.
2. Supply them with the basic questionnaire in advance. This saves time filling it in when you could be talking to each other, and acts as a joint reminder for you both during the interview.
3. Take along the suggested set of items (page 27) to help you record the interview.

## INTERVIEWING RELATIVES

4. Always be polite and restrained. Even if this is a relative who diddled your parents out of money 50 years ago, he or she could be a source of information that you cannot get elsewhere. Do not let your opinions colour your judgements. If you chance upon a subject which distresses or alarms the relative, let it drop. The most common example is illegitimacy, which is certainly not a modern phenomenon. You must respect their wishes if they do not wish to reveal something — but you will be aware of this skeleton in the cupboard, and may be able to investigate it more elsewhere.
5. Frame your questions in an open-ended way. This means asking questions in a way which cannot be answered by a simple 'yes', 'no' or similarly short response, which could result in you missing some vital information. So, instead of commenting 'So that was the end of Aunt Hattie', you might ask 'What contact did you have with Aunt Hattie after that?'

## BASICS QUESTIONNAIRE

Your current name, and any previous surnames

___

Spouse's name ___

Date and place of birth ___

Occupation ___

Spouse's date and place of birth ___

Spouse's occupation ___

Date and place of marriage ___

Children's names and dates of birth ___

Children's spouse's names and places of marriage ___

Same details for father _____

Same details for mother _____

Same details for their parents _____

Any other information which you feel may be useful _____

Going through events chronologically is usually best as it gives the conversation some structure. The following guidance on likely topics covered may help you.

**Childhood:** Place, date of birth; names of parents, brothers and sisters, other relations such as aunts and uncles, and any other people who shared the house. Their birth dates.

**School:** Friends, achievements, further study at college.

**Happy memories:** Perhaps holidays, Christmas, sports.

**Unhappy memories:** Funerals, illnesses, wartime memories.

**Military service:** Rank, location, experiences.

**Career:** Ambitions, qualifications, jobs, locations, colleagues.

**Marriage:** Early loves, location of meeting future spouse, first impressions. Location of wedding, guests, speeches, relationship with in-laws. Honeymoon. (If applicable: divorce.)

**Children:** Names, birth dates, schooldays, holidays, games, occupations.

**Community:** Addresses lived at and dates of moving. Societies joined. Friendships. Items owned (e.g. cars, bicycles).

Allow your relative time to think and answer; do not try to push or prompt them. Be aware that they may find

## INTERVIEWING RELATIVES

the process tiring, and be prepared to come back, or telephone them at a later date. Indeed, you will invariably get more useful information if you wait a few weeks and talk to the relative again, as memory is a peculiar thing and once the pool of remembrance is stirred some memories take longer than others to drift to the surface.

It may help to be forthcoming about your own life, as this will allow them to relax and pause for breath a little. It is also human nature to respond when given information with some story or comment about your own experience. So a brief outline of your career, or your children's hobbies, could encourage an interesting response. A small gift such as flowers or a bottle of wine helps ensure a friendly reception and is a nice gesture of thanks to people whose help you need.

One very useful piece of equipment is a small, portable cassette tape recorder with a plug-in or built-in microphone. A tape recording of the interview will provide a back-up for your notes. Unless you are highly proficient at shorthand, you will never note down everything said at the interview and will spend the whole time with your head down making notes!

Small recorders are best because some people find being tape-recorded rather intimidating, and will feel inhibited. A small piece of equipment will be less obtrusive. That said, never try to conceal the recorder: you must ask their permission first. Apart from being very rude, it would be difficult to operate it without their knowledge, and if they found out accidentally, you would probably lose their co-operation in any further research.

Make sure you have a plentiful supply of blank cassettes and back-up batteries, and that you know how to work the tape recorder. As each tape is used, label it carefully and remove the plastic tabs on the cassette casing so that it cannot be recorded over.

## INTERVIEWING RELATIVES

Resist any temptation to take a video camera along. Such equipment is expensive, complicated to operate while trying to conduct an interview, and is not likely to put anyone at ease.

Take a camera to photograph your interviewee (provided that they do not object). This will be a useful record for the future and could prove helpful when you are speaking to other relatives, who may not have seen that family member for many years.

Leave a stamped, self-addressed envelope. Your relative may track down other documents to forward to you, or be able to remember more things after you have left and wish to contact you. Bringing along identification also helps to reassure older people who may be a little afraid of a stranger, particularly if you ask searching questions about the past. They may be able to provide some of the following:

* Birth, marriage and death certificates
* Letters
* An old diary. (These are rarely kept but appointments diaries are more commonly found, especially if one partner was active in business)
* Books. May have inscriptions on the front page or may have been awarded as a school prize
* A family Bible. It used to be a custom to record births, deaths and marriages in a Bible which would be handed down through the generations. Your relative may have one, or know who it was passed to
* Newspaper cuttings (particularly of obituary notices)
* Medals
* Memorabilia such as receipts, tickets and letters
* Photographs. These should be photocopied, and if you have the resources, re-photographed. Never write on the back of photographs as the print will eventually show through: write the details of who is in the picture and when it was taken on a sticky label, and attach this to the back

## INTERVIEWING RELATIVES

Keep calm, take notes and when you get home read through them, making a separate note of particularly interesting points that you wish to follow up. Write or type out the interview while it is fresh in your mind. Be careful not to omit anything important or to change the emphasis of any comments made; they could lead you off the scent later on. File your notes and the cassette(s) of the interview.

You may find you get confused about inter-family relationships such as what makes a first cousin once removed. The chart on the facing page will help clarify this. Copy its structure but replace the symbols with names of the appropriate people in your family.

Of course you may have relatives on your list who live too far away to be visited, or have even moved abroad. Your best option is to contact them by letter explaining who you are and what you are trying to do, and ask them to fill in the basic questionnaire, adding as much extra information as they can remember. From this, you will be able to identify leads to follow up through subsequent letters. Remember to keep a copy of any letter you send, as the reply may be in the form of a list of answers to consecutive questions in your letter. So you need a copy of the original letter to make sense of the answers!

It is only fair to send the return postage fee with each set of questions. You can do this with an international postal order, or, better, international reply coupons (IRCs). You can purchase these at the post office, and the recipient exchanges them for sufficient stamps to mail their reply. You will need to buy at least three coupons to allow enough for air mail postage — and remember this only allows for 10 g or one sheet of A4 paper, so you may need more. IRCs are not usable in South Africa, which has been expelled from the International Postal Union.

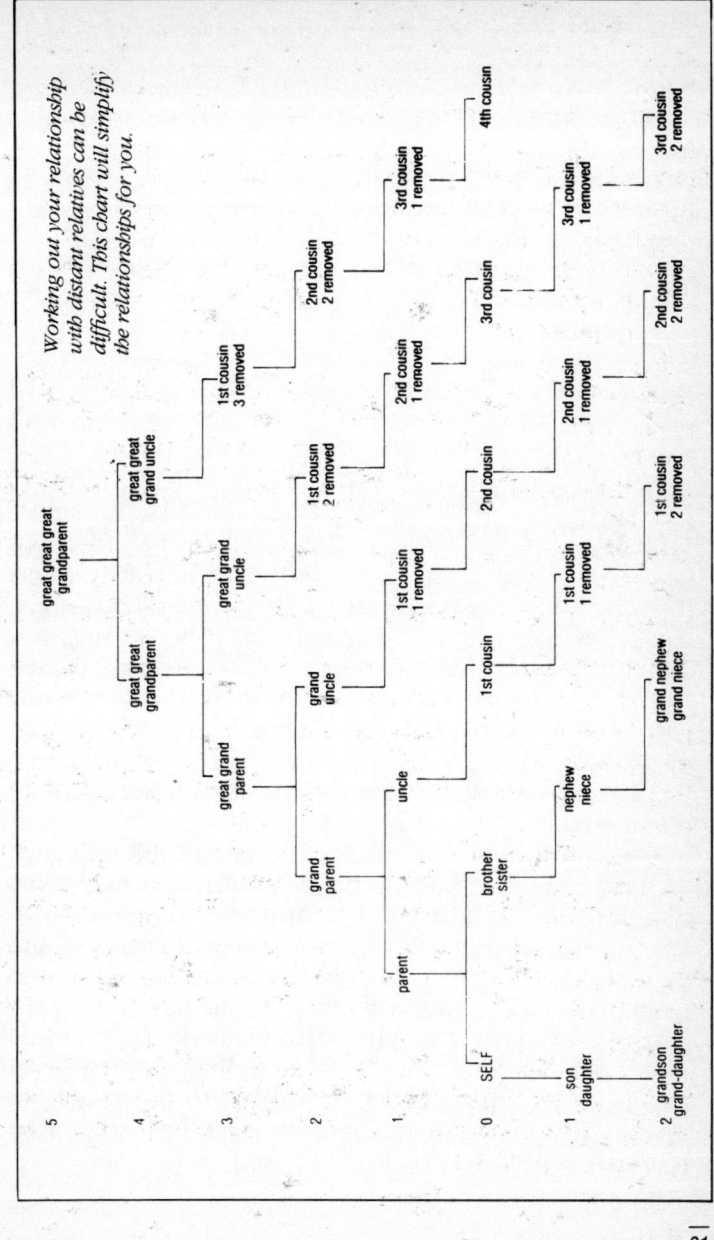

## INTERVIEWING RELATIVES

> **INTERVIEW CHECKLIST**
> 1. Pens, pencils and paper
> 2. Small tape recorder with spare batteries and blank cassettes
> 3. Relevant photographs and other useful documents
> 4. Small gift
> 5. Some form of identification
> 6. Self-addressed and stamped envelope
> 7. Camera

## OBTAINING AND EXAMINING FAMILY RECORDS

Boxes of papers collected from attics, sideboards and cellars could prove of great value to you in two ways. First, they may well include copies of birth and marriage certificates and other official documents, saving you the time and expense of locating these yourself. Second, they will provide countless tiny insights into the lives of the people mentioned.

For example, are the bride and groom holding hands in the wedding photograph, or do they look formal and strained? Are there any receipts detailing building work on the home which would provide you with an address, an idea of the size of the property, and of how prosperous the relatives involved were? Receipts, legal documents and other paperwork are always dated and often show an address as well as a name. This could save you months of toil in tracking down such details. Newspaper records such as wedding reports and obituaries are often kept by someone in the family — and often stored in some long forgotten biscuit tin or shoebox. Don't overlook any possibility that will keep you on the trail.

## Chapter 4

# CIVIL RECORDS

The next step after interviewing your relatives, as you put together the picture of your ancestry, is simple and logical. You need to obtain copies of the birth or baptism certificates of the key relatives in the line. Each of these will name at least one parent, usually both, and armed with this name you can find a marriage certificate (unless the child was illegitimate, in which case for the moment you can only follow the female line of descent). Similar research should turn up the death certificate.

You should be able to trace back through the family tree as far as 1837 using this method. From 1 July of that year all births, marriages and deaths in England and Wales were legally required to be registered. (Scotland joined the system in 1855.) Indexes of all registrations are open to public inspection. Those for England and Wales are stored at St Catherine's House in London (burials are indexed at nearby Alexandra House). For Scotland they are at New Register House, in Edinburgh. For events in Southern Ireland (all of Ireland until 1921), contact the Registrar General in Dublin. Northern Ireland records from 1921 are at Oxford House in Belfast. For records in the Isle of Man, you will need to contact the General Registry in Douglas, and for the Channel Islands, the source is the Société Jersiase (postal enquiries only). Addresses for all these offices are in the address list at the back of this book.

Whichever location you are visiting, arrive early, as you may need to allocate a viewing machine to yourself,

## CIVIL RECORDS

and at lunch times and in the summer all these offices tend to get crowded. In fact, there is very little point trying to undertake research in your lunch hour, you just won't have enough time. You are better advised to make a morning or day of it, and get there early.

Births, marriages and deaths are recorded in separate indexes, colour coded *red* for births, *green* for marriages and *black* for deaths. These record the full name, registration district, volume and page reference for locating the original document — which you will need to see to determine the parentage. Each record is divided into four quarters, comprising three months ending on the last day of March, June, September and then December. So the records for March 1850 are in the March 1850 quarter, while those for April would be in the June quarter.

Records for some very full quarters are divided alphabetically. If you are having trouble locating a volume make sure you are checking every shelf; in the London office, for example, there are three levels of shelving, with only the middle one at eye level. If you still can't find it, someone else is probably using it and you will have to wait.

You need all the details listed above to order a copy of the certificate you require (there is a charge for this). You do this by filling in an application form. You should be able to pick up the certificate within three days, but you can expect to wait longer if the document is to be posted to you. There are professional searchers who will work on your behalf tracing these records, and because many of them are regular visitors to these records offices, their charges might compare reasonably with those of the administration, especially considering how quickly the professionals can get results. They may carry out your research and order the copied document, picking it up on their next visit a few days later: so you receive it much faster than through official channels.

## BIRTH CERTIFICATES

Like the other certificates, birth certificates are dated on the day they are registered, which could be some time after the event occurred (so you may have to check more than one quarter to find what you are looking for). In 1875 registration became compulsory and a penalty was introduced for registrations made more than 42 days after the birth. As a result, some parents who were late registering adjusted the birth date to avoid paying a fine.

### BIRTH CERTIFICATES STATE:

1. Date and place of birth
2. Name
3. Sex
4. Full name of father
5. Full name of mother, including maiden name (from 1911 only)
6. Father's occupation
7. Signature of registrant
8. Date of registration
9. Signature of registrar
10. Name entered after registration (if not given at time — usually the first name)

Names may differ from what you are expecting to find: illiteracy was high in the nineteenth century, so a name mumbled to the registrar was often not checked by the parents as they left the office.

The obvious things to invariably double-check are names beginning with Mc and Mac, but if you are having trouble finding a birth certificate use your imagination to come up with some possible mis-spellings or mis-hearings of the name. If it starts with a vowel, an H may have been added — and you can bet that if the name begins with an H, that letter was omitted! First names and surnames are frequently reversed, so that Bernard Henry could be written as Henry Bernard.

After 1875, the father of an illegitimate child could only be named on the birth certificate with his consent. So before then, even if his name appeared on the certificate, the real father may have denied parentage, or been unaware of the offspring. Inclusion of the time of birth usually indicates a multiple birth: more than one child was born of the mother that day — although the infant mortality rate was so high, this may be the only indication of the sibling's short life.

## MARRIAGE CERTIFICATES

The great thing about marriage certificates is that because both parties have to be named, there is less likelihood of the genealogist being misled. Do not expect marriage dates to be prior to birth dates of any children. Couples quite often waited until after the birth of a child before tying the knot. Until modern times, a very high proportion of brides were pregnant at the time of their marriage.

### MARRIAGE CERTIFICATES STATE:

1. Date
2. Both parties' names and surnames
3. Ages
4. Status (bachelor, spinster, etc.)
5. Rank or profession
6. Residence of both parties
7. Full names of both fathers
8. Fathers' occupations

Beware of taking the ages noted too seriously as '21' and 'of full age' both mean 21 or over. You can easily authenticate a marriage certificate by checking the names of both spouses in the index for that quarter, and if the marriage reference numbers match up, you can be pretty sure you have the correct certificate.

Missing fathers' details may indicate illegitimacy, or that the parent was dead (or that the church official was negligent!)

## DEATH CERTIFICATES

Death certificates can be useful if you do not know where the ancestor was living in the later years of his or her life. Most people die at home, and so the place of death is likely to be an address where the deceased lived for a number of years. The address is also useful in checking Census Returns.

### DEATH CERTIFICATES STATE:

1. Place and date of birth
2. Full name
3. Sex
4. Age
5. Occupation
6. Cause of death
7. Signature, description and residence of informant
8. Date of registration
9. Signature of registrar

Once you have a location and date for the death, you can try to track down any obituaries which appeared in the local paper at the time. If you know where the deceased was living at around this time, but the address on the death certificate is different, they may have been visiting relatives — giving you another clue to follow up, as it could be where the family moved from.

Be wary of the age given: it may well be inaccurate and is no guide to the date of birth. The informant's details are well worth noting as this person is very likely to have been a relative. With luck you are now armed with your sets of names and addresses, and can turn your attention to the Census Returns.

## CENSUS RETURNS

A census has been conducted every ten years in Great Britain since 1801, although the first three censuses contain little information of value as they were little more than a head count. From then on, however, the data gathered is more comprehensive, and if you can trace a reference to an ancestor in a census you should be able to gather some interesting facts about his or her life. The key is to find where he or she would have been living in the year a census was made.

The records from 1841 onwards are stored at the public record offices in London and Edinburgh (a charge is made to study Scottish records). Irish records before 1901 were destroyed in 1922. You will need a Reader's Ticket from the Enquiry Office or a day pass at the door to view the English records.

When they reach 100 years of age they are made available for public inspection. (In Scotland, 1891 records are already open for inspection.) Researchers can purchase copies, or, more commonly, study them on microfilm at local libraries and record offices. There are helpful notices at the offices explaining how to locate and examine the correct microfilm.

## MICROFILM

As you travel to offices in search of certain documents, you are bound to come across records, usually indexes, stored on microfilm. This comes in a reel which fits onto a spindle of a microfilm viewing machine. The film is run through a frame and onto another spindle. Both spindles have handles which you turn to move the film, which is viewed on a screen in front of you. Although using microfilm machines can be a bit fiddly at first, just watch other people for a while, then thread on the film and have a go. It is easier than it sounds — and you will soon forget any troubles with the equipment as you enjoy discovering the documents you have come to see. Don't forget you may have to come back to re-examine a particular document, so always keep notes of any file numbers so that you can locate them quickly.

## CONTENTS OF CENSUS

With a few exceptions, the census gathered the following information, hand written onto printed forms:

1. Name of place and parish, and whether it was a hamlet, village, town or borough
2. Name or number of house and street
3. Names of people present on the night of the census (held in spring)
4. Relationship of each of these people to the head of the household
5. Matrimonial status

## CIVIL RECORDS

6. Age and sex
7. Rank, profession or occupation
8. Birthplace (Y for country of present residence, S for Scotland, I for Ireland, F for foreign parts)
9. Whether the person was blind, deaf or dumb

The enumerators marked '/' at the end of each household, and '//' at the end of each building.

So if you have an address that is correct for an 01 year, you have a reasonable chance of finding a reference to your ancestor. Look at the census returns for neighbouring streets to look for other relatives, and to get an impression of what the area was like by the occupations stated and the numbers resident in each house.

You should also check for entries made in the surnames of married daughters (perhaps her parents lived in the house?), as well as entries made in the wives' maiden names. If you are looking for a home town of the next generation back, look for servants' details. Servants often travelled with a family moving from its original homestead. Watch out for spelling variants as literacy levels were low and enumerators were probably in a hurry to complete their allocation of addresses on the day.

If you cannot find the name of a person you expected to be resident in the house in that year, it does not necessarily mean they had left. The form only records names of people *present on the night of the census*. So people in service, prison, school or hospital would not be noted. Another complication here is that the street name or boundary may have changed — so it would have been covered in a different part of the census. You can check this by noting down the names of neighbours, and finding if they can be traced as expected a decade later. If they can, your family moved away during that period.

Some occupations were abbreviated in the census return. Examples are:

**Ag. Lab.**  Agricultural labourer
**App.**  Apprentice
**Dom.**  Domestic servant
**H.**  Head of household
**Lab.**  Labourer
**N.K.**  Not known
**Serv.**  Servant

Records for 1891 become available in 1992. However, if you desperately need to see records from a census not yet released, you can request them, but you will need to tell the Census Office the correct name and address of the person. They will only search for these details, so if you get it wrong, they won't release the document. You must also promise not to use the information for litigation, and provide evidence that you are a direct descendant of the person named, or acting on behalf of such a person. If they succeed in finding the record you request, they will only tell you the age and place of birth of the people concerned. Clearly, since this search involves a fee, and you have to be so precise in your briefing, this is really a last resort if you can't trace a birth date any other way.

The dates of each census were: 6 June 1841, 30 March 1851, 7 April 1861, 2 April 1871, and 3 April 1881. There is a special magic in knowing that the details stored on the microfilm you are studying were collected on the evenings of these specific dates. It is fun to picture the scene and try to decipher a little more information from the bare details of the form.

## Chapter 5

# PARISH RECORDS

After you have consulted the civil records, as described in the previous chapter, you are likely to need to move further back in time and check on parish registers and other church documents. The church was a much more powerful force in the past than it is today. It was the centre of the local community and responsible for quite a lot of area administration before the development of local government. Some historical background is helpful here for a proper understanding of what parish registers are and how to use them.

In 1538 Thomas Cromwell, chief minister to Henry VIII, announced that every wedding, baptism and burial in each parish should be recorded. However, he did not specify exactly what should be recorded so information can vary. As notes were written in fragile paper books, the original records have not survived well: less than 700 registers from 1538 remain from an estimated total of 11,000 parishes.

A decree in 1597 that all records be updated onto parchments was poorly worded and allowed clerics to read it as instruction to copy 40 rather than 60 years' records. In the meantime, in 1598 it was decreed that transcripts of the parish registers should be sent to the relevant bishop every year. These bishops' transcripts now give the genealogist a second chance to find a birth, marriage or death if the parish records are incomplete. Inevitably, human nature being what it is, they can also contain transcription errors which take you off the trail!

As you can tell, unless you are lucky, parish records were rather idiosyncratic until standard forms were introduced in 1753 and again in 1812.

# DATES

In 1582 most of the Continent adopted the new-style Gregorian calendar, in which new year started on 1 January. Scotland adopted this in 1660, but until 1751 England still worked with the old-style Julian calendar, in which the new year began on 25 March. This was divided into four quarters, used to denote the date of due payments, ends of tenancies, etc. The days were Lady Day (25 March — traditionally the day on which fairs for hiring servants took place); Midsummer Day (24 June); Michaelmas (29 September — the Feast of St Michael); and Christmas Day (25 December). In Scotland before the new calendar was adopted the equivalent days were Candlemas (2 February); Whit Sunday (15 May); Lammas (1 August) and Martinmas (11 November).

Clearly during the period where two calendars were in operation the potential for confusion was strong. Some registrars recognised this inconsistency and recorded both dates, e.g. 24 January 1734/35 (one year in the old style, the other in the new style).

The switch to the new-style calendar in 1751 meant that the year began on 25 March and ended on 31 December, with 11 days removed altogether during September. Bankers did not like having days taken away from them, so they insisted on retaining those 11 days, which is why the financial year runs until 5 April.

**PARISH RECORDS**

Nobody ever had the nerve to challenge the financial world and bring the two years together!

Sometimes, particularly on early documents, the date refers to the period within the reign of the monarch, as in 'on the ninth day of January in the tenth year of the reign of our Gracious Queen Elizabeth'. Obviously this means you will need to check when the reign of that monarch commenced. The following chart shows the starting dates of each reign.

## KINGS AND QUEENS

| Monarch | Reign started |
|---|---|
| William I | 25 Dec 1066 |
| William II | 26 Sept 1087 |
| Henry I | 5 Aug 1100 |
| Stephen | 26 Dec 1135 |
| Henry II | 19 Dec 1154 |
| Richard I | 3 Sept 1189 |
| John* | 27 May 1199 |
| Henry III | 28 Oct 1216 |
| Edward I | 20 Nov 1272 |
| Edward II | 8 July 1307 |
| Edward III | 25 Jan 1327 |
| Richard II | 22 June 1377 |
| Henry IV | 30 Sept 1399 |
| Henry V | 21 March 1413 |
| Henry VI | 1 Sept 1422 |
| Edward IV | 4 March 1461 |
| Edward V | 9 April 1483 |
| Richard III | 26 June 1483 |
| Henry VII | 22 Aug 1485 |
| Henry VIII | 22 April 1509 |
| Edward VI | 28 Jan 1547 |
| Lady Jane Grey | 27 June 1553 |
| Mary I | 6 July 1553 |

| Monarch | Reign started |
|---|---|
| Philip and Mary | 25 July 1554 |
| Elizabeth I | 17 Nov 1558 |
| James I | 24 March 1603 |
| Charles I | 27 March 1625 |

*(Commonwealth Interregnum 1649–1660)*
| | |
|---|---|
| Charles II | 30 Jan 1649 |
| James II | 6 Feb 1685 |

*(Interregnum 12 Dec 1688–12 Feb 1689)*
| | |
|---|---|
| William III and Mary | 13 Feb 1689 |
| William III | 28 Dec 1694 |
| Anne | 8 March 1702 |
| George I | 1 Aug 1714 |
| George II | 11 June 1727 |
| George III | 25 Oct 1760 |
| George IV | 29 Jan 1820 |
| William IV | 26 June 1830 |
| Victoria | 20 June 1837 |

After this the use of regnal years ceased.

* During King John's reign, the regnal year was calculated from Ascension Day.

Remember too, if your work leads to any American sources, that in the U.S. dates are written in a different order, so that while you would write 10 December 1990 as 10/12/90, Americans would note it as 12/10/90, putting the number of the month first.

# BAPTISMS

Baptism records note the date, Christian names of the child, parent's Christian names plus father's surname — mother's surname for illegitimate children — home town or village, father's profession, and who conducted the baptism.

Parish registers noted baptisms, not births, and the chief reasons for a baptism not being conducted would be that the parents were non-conformists, Quakers, Jews or Roman Catholics. Children born away from home might well be taken back to the family parish to be baptised. Sometimes baptisms were carried out on quite old children because their parents could not afford the fee at the time of birth.

## MARRIAGES

Parish marriage records give the names of both parties, the groom's occupation, their parishes and their status (i.e. spinster, widow, bachelor, widower). If you can't find a record of a marriage in the groom's parish, look at the bride's parish — the ceremony is more likely to have been conducted there.

Clandestine marriages are another problem the genealogist faces in research into the seventeenth and eighteenth centuries. Many couples chose to avoid the hassle and expense of having banns read and licences bought, and sneaked off to places — marriage shops really — where a parson would marry them without asking too many questions. In return, no one checked out the clergyman's credentials too carefully either! Actually sometimes they were genuine parsons who were prepared to officiate at marriage without going to the bother of meeting the official requirements.

The practice was rife, sometimes for a genuine elopement and in other cases with one partner under duress or so gullible they did not realise what was going on. Naturally a clandestine marriage provided an excellent opportunity for bigamists to take their vows without being challenged. Registers of such marriages can be found at the Public Record Office and some County Record Offices.

In 1754 Parliament passed an act intended to prevent clandestine marriages. All marriages were to be performed in a parish church or designated parochial chapelry (apart from those involving Quakers and Jews, who kept perfectly good records anyway). The marriage had to be recorded in a special register on standard forms which were signed by the officiating minister, the bride and groom, and two witnesses. Always make a note of these witnesses as they are quite likely to have been relatives, too.

The marriage had to be preceded by the calling of banns or by purchasing a licence from a bishop, both of which notified an intention to marry. Banns were called and registered in the parishes of both parties. The banns can sometimes provide valuable information about the whereabouts of ancestors. Remember: finding a mention that banns were read does not necessarily mean the marriage took place.

Scotland was not affected by the law, and indeed marriage by cohabitation was recognised here until 1939. This explains the popularity of famous places such as Gretna Green in Scotland for instant marriages.

## MARRIAGE LICENCES

A couple would obtain a marriage licence, allowing the ceremony to take place without the reading of banns, if both were away from their usual residence, or did not wish to wait three weeks for the banns to be called. Soldiers and sailors who were likely to be called away at short notice often purchased marriage licences. There was also a snob value in avoiding having the banns read,

## PARISH RECORDS

as it publicised what some families preferred to keep a private matter.

Obtained from the bishop of the diocese, licences included names, residences, status (e.g. widow), ages, parishes and for minors, parents and their consent, plus the location where the marriage was to take place. Friends of relatives would provide assurances that they would ensure the couple would marry in a specified church or chapel. These were called bonds, and were kept with the licence itself. These documents are kept in Diocese Registry Offices or Civil Register Offices. Many have been indexed.

## BURIALS

Burial records can be a bit sketchy but you might be lucky and find a reference saying 'son of ...' or 'widow of ...' which will give you a new lead.

## USING PARISH REGISTERS

Up until 1754 many parish registers were not divided into baptisms, marriages and burials — all three were simply lumped together in the order they happened. So you may have to search scrupulously hard for the reference you seek. You will also find that until quite recently all parish records were handwritten. Early documents in particular can be very difficult to decipher until you become more accustomed to the script. All you can do is read the easy words and get familiar with how individual letters looked.

# NON-CONFORMIST RECORDS

Ancestors who were not followers of the Church of England make harder work for you when tracing events in their lives.

## ROMAN CATHOLICS

Births and marriages were recorded and these registers are often still with the local parish priest. Some have been deposited with Parish or County Record Offices. If you think records about an ancestor might be with a Roman Catholic priest, write giving as much detail as possible about your request. Otherwise, contact the English Catholic Ancestor.

## JEWS

Some Jews paid to have their children recorded in local parish registers (which noted 'son' or 'daughter of a Jew'), and most synagogues have records of their congregations. Write to the synagogue in the area of your interest for details of what records are available.

## NON-CONFORMIST PROTESTANTS

Baptists, Methodists, Presbyterians, United Reform Church and Congregationalists maintained records of their own congregations. Some are now with the local record offices, but many have been kept where they were made. Again, try the appropriate local church, or the Baptist Historical Society, the Methodist Archive Collection, or the Presbyterian Historical Society.

## HUGUENOTS

Huguenot records have been deposited with the local County Record Office, and if you have no success here

## PARISH RECORDS

try the Huguenot Library. Huguenots settled in southern England and came from France, Germany and the Netherlands.

## THE INTERNATIONAL GENEALOGICAL INDEX

Great help in finding references to births and marriages is available through the International Genealogical Index (IGI). This is a massive index of millions of baptisms and marriages (but not burials) around the world. It is produced by the Church of Jesus Christ of Latter-Day Saints, more popularly known as the Mormons. They produce it to help their members posthumously baptise ancestors, as they do not recognise baptisms by other denominations.

The IGI contains someting like 30 million entries in the British section, mainly baptisms, and chiefly culled from parish registers. Not every parish register is included, however, and listings for those that are present are not always comprehensive. You should also bear in mind that, as with any details copied from the original, mistakes can occur in transcription and you might feel you should trace the original document for authentication. Despite this point, the IGI can help you shortcut the research procedure and lead you straight to the document you need.

Entries for England and Scotland are arranged by county, then by surname divided by first name, and within first names in date order. Wales, Ireland, the Isle of Man and the Channel Islands are treated as counties.

Copies of the index on *microfiche* are available from some family history societies, libraries and County Record Offices, or through branch libraries of the Church of Jesus Christ of Latter-Day Saints. Always double-check information from the IGI by obtaining or at least seeing a copy of the original register entry.

> **MICROFICHE**
>
> You will find reference in this and other chapters to indexes stored on microfiche. This is a set of sheets about 10 cm × 15 cm (4 in × 6 in), on which are stored tiny photographs of lists of names. Using the microfiche reader (which looks like a computer screen), you scan the index until you find the reference, usually a name, you are seeking. Where there is a microfiche you will find lots of guidance on how to use it, and if in doubt do not hesitate to ask the staff for help: that is what they are there for.

## THE PERCIVAL BOYD INDEX

Another, but less comprehensive (a mere seven million names!), index of English marriages and London burials is the Percival Boyd Index, stored at the Society of Genealogists. It covers the period from 1538 to 1837, and is gathered from parish registers, bishops' transcripts and marriage licences.

References are categorised by county, with men and women indexed separately. His work in the nineteenth century has since inspired a number of local and family history societies to index their parish registers, so you may be lucky and find mentions of events in your ancestors' lives fairly easy to track down. When using either index, check adjacent counties if you do not find

## PARISH RECORDS

what you are looking for — it is quite possible that some administrative problem forced a couple to go further afield to have their marriage ceremony.

If you find from one of these indexes that a parish register does hold a record you would like to see, check the register's location in a handbook by Local Population Studies called Original Parish Registers. It is likely that you will need to contact the County Record Office. If the document is not noted in the book, it has stayed with the parish authorities. You may have to visit a remote parish or record office, where the incumbents must by law permit access, but are allowed to charge some fairly reasonable fees. If you do not wish to travel to see the entry, you could try to get a copy by post. Always write first asking if this would be acceptable (don't forget to include a stamped self-addressed envelope). When you send more details include a cheque with a maximum amount entered in it to cover the incumbent's costs and time. He or she will fill in the correct sum after the research has been completed.

In Scotland the registers, kept at New Register House, also show the mother's maiden name on baptism records. However, parish registers in Scotland were not well kept and if you are hoping to find a specific one in the country you may be disappointed.

## GRAVESTONES

Once you know where an ancestor was buried, you may wish to travel to the scene to examine the inscription on the gravestone. These quite often include some exaggerated eulogies, but also information which would not be available elsewhere. Visiting a grave also gives the genealogist some sense of achievement and progress in what can be a time-consuming and isolated task.

Deaths in the gentry, clergy and merchant classes

through the thirteenth to seventeenth centuries were often commemorated with monumental brasses, sunk into the stone slab. The figures on these were only rarely representations of the deceased and should be treated with caution. The size of the surrounding to the grave, and any statuary, are excellent indicators of the status and wealth of the deceased.

Take a camera with you to photograph the grave and the church — it is nice to have some sense of location with such pictures. Photograph any inscription but make a full note of it too, in case your photos are less than perfect.

Local History Societies and Family History Societies may have records of inscriptions (called MIs — monumental inscriptions). Even if your ancestor died abroad, a tombstone may have been erected, so it is always worth checking.

---

### ARCHIVE CARE

When examining parish registers and other original documents, follow these five basic rules:

1. Do not write your notes in ink — it could spill or stain the document. Use pencils.
2. Do not eat, drink or smoke while you are in the room.
3. Never rest anything on the document, including your pencil or finger — you could stain or damage it. This rule also prevents you tracing over an entry.
4. Turn the pages carefully.
5. Leave the document exactly as you found it.

## CHECKLIST FOR LOCATING AND VIEWING PARISH RECORDS

1. Consult the IGI or some similar index first.
2. Locate parish register via a directory.
3. Contact the relevant register office to see when you can visit to view the document.
4. Note all names on the documents, including witnesses, for future reference.
5. In the case of deaths, locate the grave and note any inscriptions.

# THE POOR LAW

Vagrancy and other problems associated with the poor became widespread in the sixteenth century. From 1597 the parish was allowed to levy a rate to be used to provide relief to those in need. The Great Poor Law Act of 1601 set up a system in which two householders were nominated to be overseers for such payments. If your ancestors fell upon hard times and received support from the local community, there may be a record kept of help provided. The Poor Law system survived until 1834 when the Poor Law Reform Act transferred responsibilities from parishes to Poor Law Unions. Try the Parish or County Record Office for details of their activities.

Workhouses were introduced from 1834, and if you completely lose track of an ancestor it would be worth checking the workhouse records (stored at County Record Offices or reference libraries). Because some workhouses doubled up as hospitals, quite a few people died in workhouses, even if they had not been sent there due to poverty. The initials WH on birth or death certificates denote workhouse.

## LATIN HELP

Many parish registers started off written in Latin. These words for relationships might help you through them.

**avus:** grandfather
**caelebs:** single
**conjugata:** married woman
**femina:** woman or wife
**filia:** daughter
**filius:** son
**frater:** brother
**mariti:** married couple
**martia:** wife
**mater:** mother
**nepos:** grandchild or nephew
**nepta:** granddaughter or niece
**parens:** parent or grandparent
**proles:** descendant
**relicta:** widow
**relictus:** widower
**soror:** sister
**sponsa:** wife
**sponsus:** husband
**uxor:** wife
**uxoratus:** married
**vir:** man or husband

## THE COUNTIES OF ENGLAND

1. BEDFORDSHIRE
2. BERKSHIRE
3. BUCKINGHAMSHIRE
4. CAMBRIDGESHIRE AND ISLE OF ELY
5. CHESHIRE
6. CORNWALL
7. CUMBERLAND
8. DERBYSHIRE
9. DEVON
10. DORSET
11. COUNTY DURHAM
12. ESSEX
13. GLOUCESTERSHIRE
14. GREATER LONDON
15. HAMPSHIRE
16. HEREFORDSHIRE
17. HERTFORDSHIRE
18. HUNTINGDON AND PETERBOROUGH
19. KENT
20. LANCASHIRE
21. LEICESTERSHIRE
22. LINCOLNSHIRE (HOLLAND, KESTEVEN, AND LINDSEY)
23. MONMOUTHSHIRE
24. NORFOLK
25. NORTHAMPTONSHIRE
26. NORTHUMBERLAND
27. NOTTINGHAMSHIRE
28. OXFORDSHIRE
29. RUTLAND
30. SHROPSHIRE
31. SOMERSET
32. STAFFORDSHIRE
33. SUFFOLK (EAST AND WEST)
34. SURREY
35. SUSSEX (EAST AND WEST)
36. WARWICKSHIRE
37. WESTMORLAND
38. WILTSHIRE
39. WORCESTERSHIRE
40. YORKSHIRE (EAST, NORTH, AND WEST RIDINGS)

## THE COUNTIES OF WALES

41. ANGLESEY
42. BRECKNOCK
43. CAERNARVONSHIRE
44. CARDIGANSHIRE
45. CARMARTHENSHIRE
46. DENBIGHSHIRE
47. FLINTSHIRE
48. GLAMORGAN
49. MERIONETH
50. MONTGOMERYSHIRE
51. PEMBROKESHIRE
52. RADNOR

## THE COUNTIES OF SCOTLAND

53. ABERDEENSHIRE
54. ANGUS
55. ARGYLL
56. AYRSHIRE
57. BANFFSHIRE
58. BERWICKSHIRE
59. BUTE
60. CAITHNESS
61. CLACKMANNANSHIRE
62. DUMFRIESSHIRE
63. DUNBARTONSHIRE
64. EAST LOTHIAN
65. FIFE
66. INVERNESS-SHIRE
67. KINCARDINESHIRE
68. KINROSS-SHIRE
69. KIRKCUDBRIGHTSHIRE
70. LANARKSHIRE
71. MIDLOTHIAN
72. MORAY
73. NAIRNSHIRE
74. ORKNEY ISLANDS
75. PEEBLESSHIRE
76. PERTHSHIRE
77. RENFREWSHIRE
78. ROSS AND CROMARTY
79. ROXBURGHSHIRE
80. SELKIRKSHIRE
81. SHETLAND ISLANDS
82. STIRLINGSHIRE
83. SUTHERLAND
84. WEST LOTHIAN
85. WIGTOWNSHIRE

*If you fail to find a document in the expected county, try its next-door neighbour; the counties of England and Wales were reorganised on 1 April 1974, and Scotland followed on 16 May 1975. These maps show the original and current county names.*

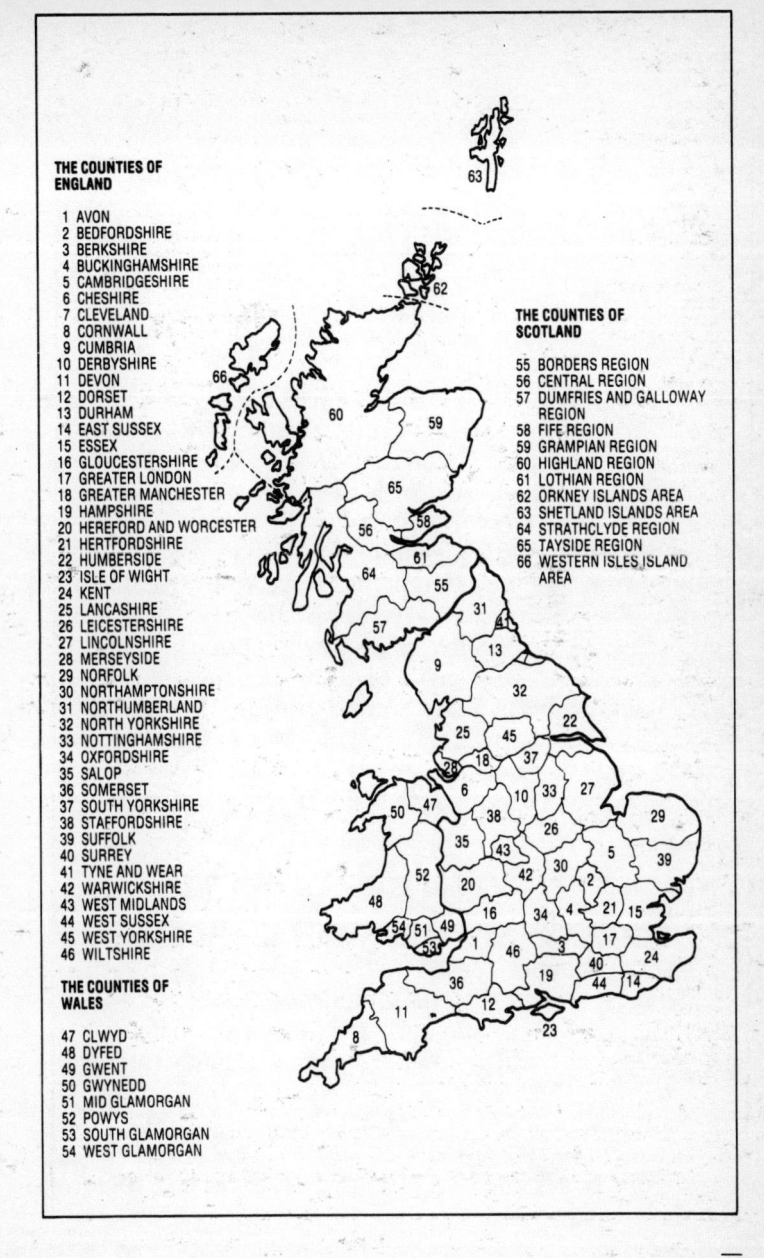

## THE COUNTIES OF ENGLAND

1. AVON
2. BEDFORDSHIRE
3. BERKSHIRE
4. BUCKINGHAMSHIRE
5. CAMBRIDGESHIRE
6. CHESHIRE
7. CLEVELAND
8. CORNWALL
9. CUMBRIA
10. DERBYSHIRE
11. DEVON
12. DORSET
13. DURHAM
14. EAST SUSSEX
15. ESSEX
16. GLOUCESTERSHIRE
17. GREATER LONDON
18. GREATER MANCHESTER
19. HAMPSHIRE
20. HEREFORD AND WORCESTER
21. HERTFORDSHIRE
22. HUMBERSIDE
23. ISLE OF WIGHT
24. KENT
25. LANCASHIRE
26. LEICESTERSHIRE
27. LINCOLNSHIRE
28. MERSEYSIDE
29. NORFOLK
30. NORTHAMPTONSHIRE
31. NORTHUMBERLAND
32. NORTH YORKSHIRE
33. NOTTINGHAMSHIRE
34. OXFORDSHIRE
35. SALOP
36. SOMERSET
37. SOUTH YORKSHIRE
38. STAFFORDSHIRE
39. SUFFOLK
40. SURREY
41. TYNE AND WEAR
42. WARWICKSHIRE
43. WEST MIDLANDS
44. WEST SUSSEX
45. WEST YORKSHIRE
46. WILTSHIRE

## THE COUNTIES OF WALES

47. CLWYD
48. DYFED
49. GWENT
50. GWYNEDD
51. MID GLAMORGAN
52. POWYS
53. SOUTH GLAMORGAN
54. WEST GLAMORGAN

## THE COUNTIES OF SCOTLAND

55. BORDERS REGION
56. CENTRAL REGION
57. DUMFRIES AND GALLOWAY REGION
58. FIFE REGION
59. GRAMPIAN REGION
60. HIGHLAND REGION
61. LOTHIAN REGION
62. ORKNEY ISLANDS AREA
63. SHETLAND ISLANDS AREA
64. STRATHCLYDE REGION
65. TAYSIDE REGION
66. WESTERN ISLES ISLAND AREA

## Chapter 6

# WILLS

Wills can provide wonderful material for the genealogist. They provide information on the wealth of the ancestor, and may name many contemporary friends and relatives as beneficiaries. If you can locate the will, from one of the addresses following, of an ancestor, do so as early in your researches as possible. In addition to valuable information, the document will take you back to the world of your ancestor — perhaps at the peak of health, sitting in an office as he decided who should receive his possessions, or maybe on his deathbed, testily barking out orders as he gained revenge on some hated relative by insulting them in his will. When you get the document, do not be afraid to enjoy this kind of speculation — it is part of the fun of genealogy.

## INFORMATION USUALLY CARRIED IN A WILL:

1. Name of testator/testatrix (male and female terms for the willmaker)
2. Testator's occupation and address
3. Dates of will, death, and granting of probate
4. Names and addresses of, and any relationship with, executors
5. Names and addresses of, and any relationship with, beneficiaries
6. Names of people excluded by definition and relationship to testator

7. Names, addresses and occupations of will witnesses. These are not allowed to be beneficiaries, so they are often legal officials and rarely family members
8. Burial instructions

Wills and Administrations for England and Wales from 1858 are stored at the Principal Probate Registry, Somerset House, The Strand, London WC2R 1LA, or where appropriate at the Borthwich Institute, York. Scottish wills are at the Scottish Record Office, HM General Register House, Edinburgh EH1 3YY.

Wills are indexed and these lists give basic facts about the deceased, the names and addresses of executors or administrators and their relationship to the deceased. For a small charge you can view the will itself and obtain a photocopy. This is a marvellous document to add to your files — do not miss a chance to get a copy.

## PRE-1858 WILLS

These were stored by Ecclesiastical Courts, and because of the complex legal system of the time there is no knowing where any particular will would have been stored. So you would have to search them all for a reference (there were about 300 Ecclesiastical Courts prior to 1858). These courts were part of a structure as shown in the box on the following page:

There were courts of varying kinds at each of these levels. The most important by far was the Prerogative Court of Canterbury (PCC), and fortunately for the researcher indexes to the wills proven at it from 1383 to 1700 have been produced. In addition, some wills made between 1750 and 1800 have been indexed by the Society of Genealogists, who will search for specific names in them for a small fee. So whichever is the more appropriate index should be consulted first, and if you have no luck try the County Record Offices.

# WILLS

> ## THE ECCLESIASTICAL STRUCTURE
> 
> ★ A parish is a small unit with a vicar or rector. The parish took over administration from the manorial courts in the sixteenth and seventeenth centuries.
> ★ Groups of up to 12 parishes form the rural deanery, headed by the dean who is usually also a minister of one of the parishes.
> ★ Groups of these in turn were part of an archdeanery, headed by an archdeacon.
> ★ Archdeaneries in a given area formed the Diocese, led by a bishop.
> ★ Finally in England and Wales the Dioceses form separate provinces, of which there are three: Canterbury, York and Wales.

Welsh wills proved before 1858 are at the National Library of Wales, Aberystwyth. Scottish wills prior to 1858 were held at Sheriff Courts and most were passed on to the Scottish Record Office, which maintains an index of them at General Register House in Edinburgh. In Ireland the Prerogative Court was that of the Archbishop of Armagh. Most wills held in file were destroyed in 1922, but some indexes have been compiled, and post 1858 wills are held in the Principle Probate Registry in Dublin.

A Scottish man can only dispose of all his estate if he is not survived by his wife or children, although he can still distribute a proportion of it. The Scots do not have wills, only testaments.

Married women who took their vows prior to 1883 could not make a will without their husbands' consent. Others forbidden to make wills were children (boys from 14, girls from 12), lunatics, heretics, apostates, prisoners and slaves.

The difference between a will and a testament is that the former deals with real estate, the latter with personal property.

Apart from its intrinsic interest, a will usually makes perfectly clear the family relationships of the time — which can be invaluable in clearing confusion on whether someone was a cousin, half-brother or whatever. It can also be a beautifully written parchment document — or a few scrawled notes. The willmaker's possessions may be bequeathed to one person, or scattered more widely — which sometimes allowed an opportunity to state a few opinions about relatives and friends to be read out once the deceased was safely in his grave! Making lots of bequests involves the full listing of the deceased's property, which is invariably a fascinating document well worth having. If the person was a tradesman, his tools or stock will often be listed.

If there was no will, some members of the family would probably have applied to be executors through Letters of Administration. These would include the full names and addresses of all the proposed executors.

In all cases, once you start searching an index for a will it is well worth looking for all wills made in the family surname. That way you can be sure of seeing a number of records, some of which may steer you to other parts of the family.

## Chapter 7

# NEWSPAPERS

Local and sometimes national newspapers can be a wonderful source of information, direct or background, about your ancestor and the area he or she lived in. There is a long-established saying in the newspaper trade that 'names sell papers', meaning that anyone who thinks their name appears in a publication wants to see a copy of it. This trait of human nature encourages papers to mention as many local people as possible. Study of some publications reveals they carried as many as 300 names in one edition.

Local newspapers started to appear round about 1750, but really started to boom during the nineteenth century. The chances of you finding a mention of an ancestor in the local paper of the day, therefore, are actually quite good. When you widen the search to include relatives' and friends' names, the odds are even better. But even if you don't find a specific reference, you can enjoy the satisfaction of reading stories your ancestors read or heard about.

The British Newspaper Library at Colindale in north London has an extensive collection of newspapers as far back as 1801. Earlier papers are stored in the Burney Collection at the British Library. Many county libraries have a set of newspapers from the region. If you want to look at national newspapers of the day, copies of *The Times* are stored on microfilm at many large reference libraries. If you cannot find the issue you are looking for, you could also contact the paper direct — they may have an archive of back issues.

It is best to start looking for issues of the paper at dates when you know for certain which area your ancestor was living in. That way you know for sure that this is news that affected their lives. You can also use local papers as a gamble if searching for a reference to a birth, wedding or death. You will have to guess the period when the event should have occurred, and spend a lot of time going through each issue. Take care to scan every page carefully. The text was sometimes quite small and the layouts not as clear as those of today.

When you get a copy of the local newspaper, study it in detail. Start with the personal columns looking for mentions of births, deaths, marriages and divorce. Death notices and obituaries usually carry personal details about the deceased, and give names of associated persons who will include relatives. Perhaps an inquest was to be held — which gives you another lead to follow.

Accounts of weddings were restricted to families of high social standing, but when they do appear contain a wealth of detail including the list of guests and descriptions of clothes worn. Don't neglect to read the advertisements, as these could include notices for sale of houses or possessions, or of tradesmen offering services.

Major local events such as fires or murders are bound to be reported too — so if you know something important happened to your ancestor's family at a certain time, keep looking, as the story should be carried somewhere. Perhaps you know your ancestor was a miller, but moved away from the area. If this was due to some disaster like the collapse of a grain store or mill, you have found a possible explanation for him leaving the area. Accounts of court trials are often very thorough, and you may discover all kinds of facts!

# Chapter 8

# SERVICE AND PROFESSIONAL RECORDS

It is very likely that at least one of your ancestors was a member of the armed forces. Provided you have a name (and hopefully a regiment, ship name or other relevant detail) you may be able to trace a record of him.

## ARMY RECORDS

From 1660 on, records were kept of armed forces, but not of high quality — you will probably have to wait until after 1829 for anything really useful. Hereafter the Army Lists of officers recorded place of birth, details of marriage, spouse and children, and most interestingly, a service record.

The best bet when looking for ranks other than officer are the soldier discharge papers, which cover the years 1756 to 1913. Prior to 1873, however, you will need to know the name of the regiment he served in. These records only contain details of soldiers who were discharged with a pension, so if your relative died on service or deserted, the trail goes cold. These papers include a physical description (one of the few places you will find such detail), medical record and intended place of residence. Most army records (including those from both World Wars) are at the Kew Public Record Office, where there will also be a record of any medals that may have been awarded.

For victims of either of the two World Wars, you may wish to visit war memorials in their home towns, or travel to see the war graves in France. It is a strange feeling to know that the anonymous-looking name engraved on a piece of stone is one of your ancestors, so be prepared to feel quite emotional when the moment does come.

For a view of life in the army since 1812, you may find it worthwhile visiting the Imperial War Museum library in London. This has a great deal of material including many photographs of scenes of army life. You never know, one of those faces could be your ancestor's!

## NAVAL RECORDS

The Public Record Office at Kew also holds a wide selection of naval documents. It produces an excellent range of pamphlets offering guidance on its records, which is available by post. It is well worth sending for these before actually making a visit to Kew. Among the papers you might consult are:

1. Payments to seamen and dependants 1675 to 1822.
2. Description books of naval staff, begun in 1790.
3. List of ships' crews from 1740 (giving name, rank, place of birth and age).
4. Navy Lists — officers and commissions from 1749.
5. Pay records.
6. For merchant seamen, certificates of competence and service for a variety of jobs.

## SERVICE AND PROFESSIONAL RECORDS

7. Registers of births, marriages and deaths of passengers at sea.

There are many more such records at Kew.

For the merchant navy, you could also try St Catherine's House in London for births and deaths of personnel 1837–1890, with records after that held by the Registrar General for Shipping and Seamen in Cardiff. Crew Lists from 1863 to 1913 were moved from Kew to the Maritime History Group in Canada. Some crew lists include physical descriptions, shore residence, and tell you whether the seaman could read or write.

If you lose track of, or have a gap in knowledge of, an ancestor who went to sea, you stand a good chance of tracing some information about him, provided you have a full name and some supporting details.

## ROYAL AIR FORCE RECORDS

This is the least productive of the three services in terms of service records. In general, ground staff are harder to trace than air crew. Again, records are kept at Kew, and you can make specific enquiries to the Air Historical Branch of the Ministry of Defence.

## PROFESSIONAL AND TRADE RECORDS

Many guilds (known as Livery Companies in London) have been formed over the centuries, and most still survive in some form. You are quite likely to have an ancestor who was apprenticed to some trade, and fairly good records were kept of such training. You will need

## APPRENTICESHIPS

Between 1710 and 1811 a set of apprenticeship books were kept, and these can now be found at the Public Record Office in Kew. They contain a reference to every apprenticeship, giving the name of the trainee, the name and trade of the master, and sometimes the names and residences of both fathers. Apprenticeships were often awarded by the parish to poor children. Quite often the local people were shrewd enough to set up the apprenticeship with a master in the next parish. That way, any further funding for the child came from the parish next door!

# Chapter 9

# MAPS AND LAND RECORDS

If you are seeking background information on the way of life in a particular area at a certain time, a local history society may be able to help. This can be especially useful if you do not live in the area in question, and so cannot conduct any local research of your own.

Local History Societies can cover counties, towns, or even just villages. Many produce a small pamphlet describing the changes that the area has seen and the way of life of past inhabitants. The British Association for Local History (BALH) is based at Shopwyke Hall, Chichester, Sussex. It can provide details of its activities and a list of publications. If you cannot contact a local society via the BALH, try to get a copy of its out-of-print publication *Local History Societies in England and Wales: A List* which you may be able to find at a library. Another possible source of this information is your area Public Record Office.

## MAPS

It is well worth investigating to see if there are any maps and plans showing the area at the time your ancestor

## MAPS

was alive. Some maps include names of property holders, although many do not. However, you will be able to find contemporary sites such as schools, churches and stations, and will be able to recreate some of the journeys your ancestors undertook every day. You should also discover how many original buildings remain from your ancestors' days — perhaps they were the scenes of visits or courting? Keep an eye out for old spellings of places which may have been changed over the years.

Local Record Offices are a good point to start with. They may have Enclosure Awards, of which two copies were made, one going to the County Record Office, the other to the local Clerk of the Peace — so the odds of finding such a map are halved! Estate maps can also be very useful.

The Tithe Commutation Act of 1836, which switched tithe payments (a tenth of produce going to the local church) into an annual rent based on the price of corn, resulted in the drawing of many tithe maps from 1838 to 1854. Three copies of these large scale maps were made, one now usually found at the County Record Office, another for the bishop, which may now be in the Diocesan Archives, and the last went to the Tithe Redemption Commission.

The Ordnance Survey began publishing maps in 1801, and continues to revisit areas to update its work. A wide range have been re-produced by David & Charles of Newton Abbot, Devon, and by Harry Margary of Lympne Castle, Kent.

A great many maps, including the Tithe Apportionments and Maps, are stored at the Public Record Office. You could also try the Curator of Maps at the British Museum, Great Russell Street, London WC1B 3DG for copies of some early maps, which may also be available from Alan Godfrey, 57–58 Spoor Street, Dunston, Gateshead, Tyne and Wear, NE11 9BD. Local maps of eighteenth and nineteenth century London are published by the London Topographical Society at 36 Old Deer Park Gardens, Richmond, Surrey, TW9 2TL.

# LAND RECORDS

Land ownership records have always carried a genealogical element, as land was often passed down the family and people needed to know who their ancestors were to prove that they were the rightful occupants of the land or holders of the tenancy.

## THE DOMESDAY BOOK

The most famous record of land ownership and occupancy is the Domesday Book, a survey ordered by William the Conqueror in 1086. If you are able to trace an ancestor back this far you are fortunate indeed. The survey was designed to be a register of all taxable holdings. This means it excluded lands and buildings, such as those owned by religious houses, which were exempt from taxation. Land tenure at this time was based on military service: so if you find a landowning ancestor, he may well have fought for William the Conqueror when he invaded England in 1066.

The original Domesday Book is held at the Public Record Office at Chancery Lane, London. Even if you do not expect to find an ancestor in it, it is worth having a look at its findings. You may have some idea of the size and character of a village in later years when you know it was inhabited by an ancestor. Now you may get some idea of what it grew from and how it had developed up to that time — giving you some idea perhaps of the prosperity or poverty of the region, for example.

## LAND TAX

Around 1692 land tax was introduced. Names of owners or tenants of houses and land were listed annually, and most survive at the relevant County Record Office.

## TITLE DEEDS

Title deeds are useful for filling in details of family history (especially occupation) if you can find them. Title deeds is a general term for papers detailing land and property ownership. Again, try the County Record Office (the Scottish Record Office for Scotland).

## ENCLOSURE AWARDS

Between 1760 and 1860 a great deal of land was fenced, walled or hedged in, in what has been called the Agrarian Revolution. To do this, Enclosure Awards were made by local commissioners, and you will find their records at County Record Offices. If you find your ancestor's land detailed here, you are lucky indeed. Now you can find out who all the owners and tenants were, and exactly where the lands referred to were situated, often with a map which accompanied the document notifying the decision.

## ESTATE RECORDS

You are very likely to have a number of ancestors who were labourers or servants on the estates of the nobility or landed gentry. Obviously they all had to be paid, and it was the job of the farm bailiff to keep good records of these payments and the work they covered. These documents should now be in a record office, but you may have trouble tracing one you are after if the landowner held more than one estate in different parts of the country. He would have found it easiest to keep all his records in one place, so you may have to do some detective work into his holdings.

If you know your ancestor was a labourer in one area but do not know who for, check the monuments at the local church. These will give details of the local landowners. Find the likely names for the right dates, and then check their estate records at the County Record Office.

Records of land held by the Crown are at the Chancery Lane Public Record Office or the Crown Estate Commissioners. For the Duchy of Cornwall, they are at the Estate Office in Buckingham Gate, London.

**Be prepared:** as they were legal documents, many land records were kept in Latin. You will not need to know the language to read them, but you will need a specialist book explaining the terms you come across. Try the McLaughlin Guide *Simple Latin for Family Historians* available from the Federation of Family History Societies, or *Latin for Local History* by Eileen A. Gooder (Longmans, 1979, 2nd edition).

## MANORIAL RECORDS

The church was a major landowner before parish registers were introduced, and manorial records can be a useful source of background information for these times. A department of the National Register of Archives holds most of them, including the court rolls. These record the actions of manorial courts which dealt with tenants' activities, from ownership claims after a tenant's death to misdemeanours such as not keeping houses in good repair. They were presided over by the steward.

## Chapter 10

# IMMIGRATION AND EMIGRATION

Families and individuals are more likely to move than to stay in the same place throughout their lives. Within the country, permanent movements were generally as little as 10 to 20 miles. This explains the value of checking adjacent parishes and counties if a relative 'disappears' — they probably did not go very far.

## EMIGRATION

However, if they moved abroad, the family detective faces a new challenge, tracing them in foreign climes. The expansion of the British Empire offered a number of opportunities for emigration in the nineteenth century. This was usually through a trading company, and they kept quite thorough records of personnel and business activity. They are therefore an excellent source of background material for your family history.

The Public Record Office at Kew is a good starting place as it holds numerous Colonial Office Records. It also has a chronological list of passport applications from 1795. Shipping lists usually travelled with the ship and so are usually to be found at the port of arrival. Sometimes copies survive at the port of origin too.

## IMMIGRATION AND EMIGRATION

If you know which country your ancestor went to, a good social history of that land is likely to mention the British influence and you may learn more about why the person emigrated.

## AMERICA

Indexes and passenger lists from 1800 to 1952 survive at the Central Reference Division, National Archives in Washington DC. However, they will only search for information if you already know names, port of entry, name of vessel, or some other supporting detail. Some people went to America as 'bound servants', agreeing to serve eight years in return for their passage. Their records are at the Public Record Office at Kew. You could also consult the 'AMINDEX' archive of emigrants' names at the Surname Archive.

## AUSTRALIA

Contrary to popular myth, it was not only convicts who endured the long boat journey to Australia. A remarkable census in 1828 undertaken in New South Wales and Tasmania offers many thousands of names of settlers. There is a copy on microfilm at Kew Public Record Office.

## CANADA

The great fur trading Hudson's Bay Company's records are at the Public Record Office in Kew, although you will need the company's permission to examine them. Try the 'CANINDEX' index of emigrants to Canada at the Surname Archive.

## INDIA

The India Office Library in London has application records submitted to the East India Company (who could refuse entry) prior to 1834. This power of the Company works to the genealogist's advantage because if someone went to India, they were most likely in its employ. Family influence was also often required to get a job with the East India Company, as applications outstripped demand. This will make it easier for you to trace family movements to the country.

# IMMIGRATION

Settlers have been coming to Great Britain for centuries, inspired or forced by a variety of reasons. Religious and political persecution are the chief spurs for refugees. Naturally enough such groups tended to stay together as much as possible at first, but most eventually blended in with the rest of the community. Their tracks are still evident through many names which came to Great Britain with immigrants and joined the stock of names in their new country. If you find an ancestor was an immigrant, imagine their trepidation as their boat docked in this new and strange land.

All aliens were obliged to register with the local Justice of the Peace. Their landlords were also required to inform the parish authorities if they gave lodging to aliens. You can look for these at the County and Public Record Offices.

## HUGUENOTS

Huguenots were chiefly French Protestants, although some came over from Holland and Germany. Persecuted in their homeland, they began to come to England in the early sixteenth century, and the stream continued for the next couple of centuries (in 1685 more than 40,000 arrived). They settled mainly in London (Soho and Spitalfields), ports on the south coast, and the West Country. If you had ancestors in any of these areas, they would certainly have been aware of the arrival of such foreigners. As they became assimilated into local communities, you are quite likely to have some Huguenot blood. The Huguenot Society has gathered a wealth of information about this important influence on our society.

## THE JEWS

Jews were expelled from England in 1290 and re-admitted in 1655, although they suffered many legal disabilities (such as being forbidden to own property or vote) which were not finally ended until the nineteenth century. They came from Spain, Portugal (whose Catholicism did not encourage religious tolerance), Germany and later central Europe. Although they were often in business, Jews have retained a strong sense of separate identity and are more likely than not to marry within their own culture. This means that quite thorough records of events in the Jewish community were kept and retained at local and national centres of the faith.

## Chapter 11

# THE ORIGINS OF NAMES

What's in a name?, asks Shakespeare in *Romeo and Juliet*. The answer is plenty for the family detective, who can have great fun tracking down the origin of a favourite first name in the family, and endless speculation on how a surname came into use.

## SURNAMES

The surname is your key weapon in tracing the male line back through the generations, and indeed in correctly identifying the female line. Yet, unfortunately, at all stages of research you can fall victim to a misspelt surname, and as you go further back in time, spellings of the same name would have varied greatly between people anyway — literacy was not widespread, so spelling checks were virtually non-existent. So the name Wright might be spelt Rite, Wighte, or even White if the name was misheard. Registration documents from as late as the nineteenth century even show many people who simply made their mark in the space allowed for a signature.

Furthermore, it was common to condense long surnames to fit them into the small space available on standard forms. So Hodgkinson might be written as Hgkson, or Raymundson as Ray. A contracted name would have a short wavy line penned over it to show the amendment, but these are easy to miss.

Your own surname may change as you delve into the past, and you may come across unusual surnames of people who had links with your ancestors — perhaps the maiden name of a woman who married into the family. An unusual surname is a great advantage as it is far easier to track down, say, Westcott, than sift through numerous Browns and Smiths.

Studying a surname's origin and meaning can help to furnish major clues to your ancestors' place of origin, class, nationality, occupation, and so on. Surnames came into use to distinguish between people with the same first name. Hereditary surnames did not exist before the Norman Conquest in 1066. There are five common sources of surnames: place, occupation, relationship, nickname and the natural world.

## PLACE

This is the most common root, with names such as Wood and Hill cropping up across the country, and others such as Townsend, Churchill or French being equally obvious signs of original location. A landowner might adopt the name of his village or estate as a surname. Some French place-names are still used as surnames in Britain, evidence of some connection to the Norman invasion. Beaumont and Grenfell are two examples.

## OCCUPATION

This is another very common root, although the original occupation is not always clear to us today. Carpenter, Baker and Farmer are pretty obvious, but a few trickier ones are listed below. If a name you come across seems similar, in spelling or sound, it is a fair bet that its origin is the same.

**Bowyer:** An archer, or a maker and dealer in archery bows.
**Carter:** A waggoner, sometimes a head of stables.
**Collier:** Charcoal seller, coal miner, or even sailor on a coal ship.
**Couper:** Merchant, especially of cattle and horses.
**Dexter:** A dyer.
**Fletcher:** Same as Bowyer.
**Frobisher:** Armour polisher.
**Greave:** Foreman or bailiff.
**Howard:** Derived from Hayward, which was the title of an official on every manor.
**Hind:** Servant or farm labourer.
**Hollister:** Female brothel-keeper.
**Jagger:** Hawker or pedlar.
**Lavender:** A washerwoman (from the French verb to wash, *laver*).
**Lorimer:** A maker of small pieces of ironware for horses.
**Mercer:** Haberdashery merchant.
**Reeve:** Tenant's representative.
**Scrimshaw:** Fencing master (from the French, *scremisseur*).
**Smith:** A worker in metal.
**Spencer:** Derived from dispensers of provisions.
**Sumner:** Summoner of people to appear in court.
**Sumpter:** Driver of a packhorse.
**Woodward:** Someone in charge of wood, whether it be a forest or timber.
**Wright:** Maker of things.

# RELATIONSHIPS

Endings of 'son' clearly indicate the origin of the

surname as that of the father, as do 's' endings as in Wills and Jones. This can lead to confusion as, for example, in Wales William Evans' son might be known as Wyn Williams(on). Scottish and Welsh babies were most likely to be named after the surname or, early on, the first name of their father. (So the son of Evan might be called Owen Evan, and his son might be named John Owen Evan. At first there would be an added 'ap' between each name but this practice died out.) Mothers were remembered too, sometimes, particularly if the birth was illegitimate or if the mother died in childbirth and was to be remembered posthumously. So Annis is derived from Agnes, and Marriot from Mary, and Mudd from Maud. Saints' names were popular roots, especially if the birth occurred on a well-known saint's day. Sissons derives from St Cecilia, 22 November, for example.

## NICKNAMES

The word comes from an 'eke' name, which means an 'other' name. Physical characteristics (Redhead, Armstrong) or peculiarities (Gifford means bloated, Cruikshank means lame leg) often inspired surnames. Family traits such as Brown, Long or Rouse (red-haired), or moral attributes (Good, Gay, Sweet) were also common sources.

## THE NATURAL WORLD

Animals (Bull), plants, fruits and flowers (e.g. Quince) were also likely to inspire a surname.

There are many books offering details of the meaning of different surnames, but bear in mind how much your own name could have been changed over the centuries.

# FIRST NAMES

There are a number of sources from which first names were derived: Latin, descriptions of the person, parental opinion, for example — see which of these you can spot in the list printed below! A favourite source was the Bible, which people were fairly familiar with (even if they did not read it) through sermons, preachers and so on. If a name has 'Jo' in it, it is a fair bet it is derived from Jove, or God, and has been used to praise Him.

One thing you should look out for is confusing shortenings of names to fit them into forms, as happened with surnames as we have already mentioned. Be prepared to use a little lateral thinking if a name you were expecting to find, say, as a mother on a birth certificate is not quite what you had anticipated. A little imagination can turn an odd-looking hieroglyphic into a recognisable name, for example Xpr is Christopher, and DY is Dorothy. That said, any inconsistencies should be treated with caution and you should make absolutely sure you double check the reference to authenticate the information.

Pet names were sometimes used, too, so that Henry becomes Harry, or Mary turns into Molly on an official document. Naturally enough, these pet names came into common usage as names in their own right. Sally was once a pet form of Sarah, for example. By 1700, both Henry and Harry featured in the 50 most popular names.

## ORIGINAL MEANINGS

Here are some examples which may help you appreciate why an ancestor was given a certain name:

**Adam:** red (from Hebrew)
**Agatha:** good

## THE ORIGINS OF NAMES

**Andrew:** manly (from the Greek)
**Anne** and variants such as **Ann**, **Anna**, **Annette**: Western form of the Hebrew Hannah
**Anthony:** from the Latin, Antonius
**Cecil:** blind
**Charles:** a man
**Christopher:** bearing Christ (in your heart)
**David:** 'friend' or 'darling' in Hebrew
**Eleanor**, or **Helen**: from the Latin Helena
**Francis:** a Frenchman
**George:** a farmer
**Mary:** 'wished for child' (Hebrew)
**Natalie**, **Noel**: born of baptised on Christmas Day
**Richard:** 'firm ruler'
**Stephen:** from the Greek 'crown'. The name of the first Christian martyr
**Sarah:** princess
**Thomas:** a twin

The further back into the past you travel through your family tree, the more significant the given names seem, because familiarity with the meanings of names was so much greater than it is today. Middle names are often included to please relatives who the parents do not actually want to name their child after. Certainly the middle name is often a clue to the name of an earlier or contemporary relative. If a widow or divorcée with children remarried, she often named her children with their real father's and their step-father's names to avoid losing any claim to land from their natural father.

## Chapter 12

# HERALDRY

Few sights can be more thrilling for the family detective than that of a coat of arms on a family document. It implies that your family has achieved a certain social standing, and carries with it a sense of heritage. Be cautious at first and do not assume you have discovered the family crest. The find could mean your family was among the nobility of its day — or perhaps an ancestor was merely a servant to people of a high social status!

## FAMILY CRESTS

The sporting of heraldry began in the eleventh century, inspired in part by the need to identify particular people amid the turmoil of the battlefield, and partly by the use of seals on legal documents. It certainly made a lot of sense to have flags, banners and decoration on your shield and armour to identify you. After all, it is bad enough to be wounded in a battle — but to be hit by one of your own side must be very embarrassing!

As the variety of different symbols used in heraldry grew, so a system of granting and registering arms arose. The king or queen of the time was regarded as the ultimate arbiter of whether a certain coat of arms was permitted. Once established, the coat of arms would be handed down through the male line for ever more.

## HERALDRY

Although whoever took on the coat of arms would have been of the nobility, that does not mean that we do not all have some chance of finding a family crest in our past. Fortunes change over the generations and it only takes a few inveterate gamblers or a series of misfortunes to transform a family's social status from local kingpin to obscure inhabitant. In England it tended to be the gentry who were considered eligible to carry armorial bearings. From early in the sixteenth century certain property requirements had to be met before you were allowed to use a coat of arms.

Each element in the design had its own significance, and a family motto was frequently added to the end result. What appears to us as a pretty pattern or a bizarre mix of symbols would have been much more easily discernible to the people of its time. Shields were displayed on walls, and their designs would have been as familiar as the family surname. Servants often wore clothes in the family colours, and a family seal would have echoed the coat of arms.

Designs from the fourteenth century are full of pomp and splendour, often appearing very formal. In the next century designs became more flamboyant, and early in the sixteenth century flowers and brighter colours were in vogue. Then the fashion changed to a more ordered simplicity, before the Victorians brought in more clutter and action in their day.

Yellow and white are used to indicate gold and silver respectively, and on top of these five colours are used in early designs: red, blue, black, green and purple. At first, the design would be in quarters, so that it fitted a shield and could be easily read. Each quarter would hold a certain symbol saying something about the holder of the arms. These are so numerous that they cannot be summarised here, and you will need to consult a specialist book to interpret any designs you find. Indeed as the symbols grew, so the shape of the design was changed to accommodate more and more emblems — dividing each quarter in half again.

## MOTTOS

Mottos were introduced in the fourteenth century, although they were not accepted in general usage until the seventeenth century. The motto is usually written on a scroll which is sometimes placed over the crest but more often under the arms. Usually written in Latin, mottos are generally a statement of virtue and honour, such as 'To serve with fortitude'. It is difficult to believe that our ancestors would have felt any more able than ourselves to follow the moral guidance mottos often carry!

There are plenty of publications which will tell you all you need to know about the meanings of heraldry. If you find a coat of arms on a relevant document, do follow it up — the results are always interesting and will add a lot to your family history.

The Ordinaries can be 'cotised' or 'charged'.

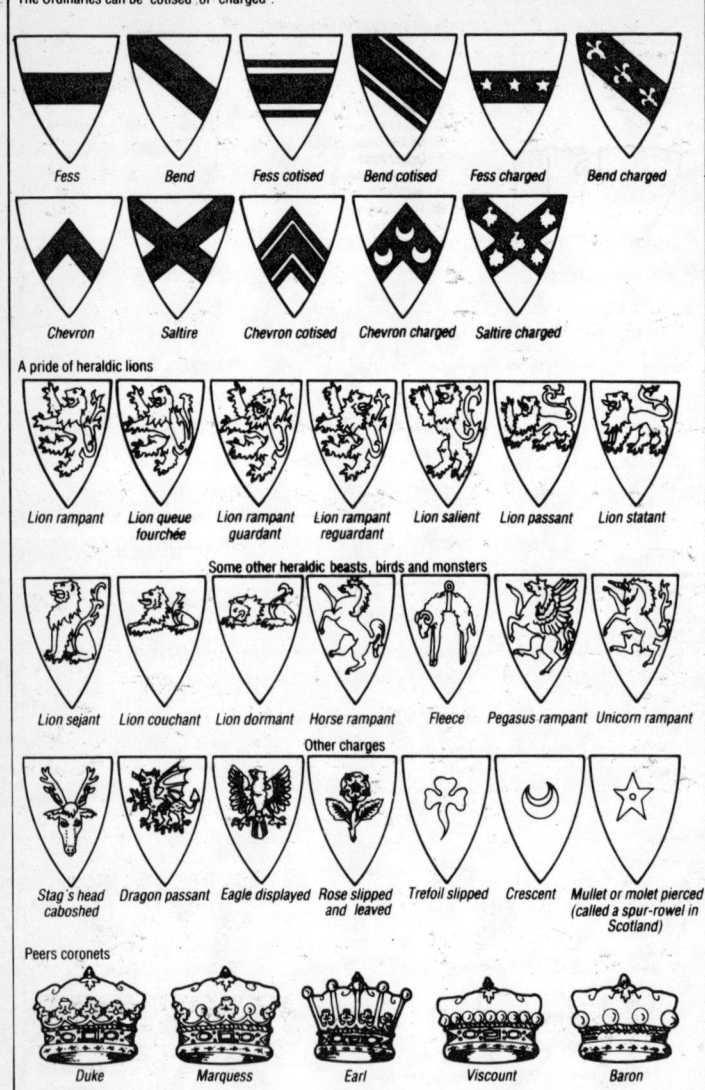

| Fess | Bend | Fess cotised | Bend cotised | Fess charged | Bend charged |

| Chevron | Saltire | Chevron cotised | Chevron charged | Saltire charged |

A pride of heraldic lions

| Lion rampant | Lion queue fourchée | Lion rampant guardant | Lion rampant reguardant | Lion salient | Lion passant | Lion statant |

Some other heraldic beasts, birds and monsters

| Lion sejant | Lion couchant | Lion dormant | Horse rampant | Fleece | Pegasus rampant | Unicorn rampant |

Other charges

| Stag's head caboshed | Dragon passant | Eagle displayed | Rose slipped and leaved | Trefoil slipped | Crescent | Mullet or molet pierced (called a spur-rowel in Scotland) |

Peers coronets

| Duke | Marquess | Earl | Viscount | Baron |

# The Basic Geometry of Heraldry

## Forms of shield

## The parts and points of an heraldic shield

A Chief
B Base
C Dexter Chief
D Sinister Chief
E Middle Chief
F Dexter Base
G Sinister Base
H Middle Base
● Honour Point
■ Fess Point
▲ Nombril (or Navel) Point

Dexter    Sinister

## Forms of line used on an heraldic shield

- Engrailed
- Invected
- Wavy (or Undy)
- Nebuly
- Indented
- Dancetty
- Embattled
- Raguly
- Dovetailed
- Potenty
- Angled
- Bevilled
- Escartelly
- Nowy
- Battle embattled (or Embattled grady)

## The shield can be divided in various ways:

Per fess or and gules | Per pale argent and vert | Per bend argent and azure | Vert a chevron or | Argent a chief gules | Or a fess sable | Paly or and azure

## Other fields used include the following:

Per salure | Bendy | Quarterly

Paly | Barry

## Among more varied fields are the following:

Gyronny | Fusily

Chevronny | Checky | Lozengy

## Chapter 13

# WRITING UP YOUR FAMILY HISTORY

Drawing up a family tree chart was explained earlier in this book. Such charts are interesting to look at but they can only carry the basic details of the lives involved. You can become so enthusiastic that you want to write a much fuller account of what you know of your ancestors' lives. Such a document will prove to be of lasting interest within and outside your family.

The trouble is, you will find yourself putting off writing such a history as your researches continue and your information grows. You may also be a little nervous of putting pen to paper. However, once you start you will most likely find penning the family story one of the most rewarding results of your efforts, and it is easier than it might appear.

The story can be written in sections. Start with your parents or grandparents and give an account of their lives from birth up to the present, or death. Try to avoid making a simple list of dates and facts and add some comment or supporting detail. For example:

'Thomas Muster was born in the Oxfordshire village of Hook Norton in 1891. His father was the local baker and business was probably quite good as the village was expanding at this time. Thomas might have been expected to join in the family business. However, he seems to have been a very spirited young man and he went to London in 1906 to join his uncle William Johnson's firm of solicitors as a clerk. The firm had offices opposite Harrods in Knightsbridge — which was in the same location as today but with smaller premises — so the street outside his workplace would have been teeming with activity. A bitter argument with his relative (still remembered in the family — apparently it was to do with the petty cash) led Thomas to leave suddenly. William Johnson clearly never forgave the boy as he left him out of his will altogether, although many other members of the family were beneficiaries. It is not clear how Thomas spent the next few years, but he may have obtained some mechanical or engineering training, because he joined up with the army in 1914, when he said he was a mechanic.'

The tale continues in this vein, noting all known events, providing supporting evidence, and stating clearly what is speculation and what is fact. You should give the authentication for each fact as a footnote at the end of each section. Quotations from newspapers, wills or other documents should be put in 'inverted commas' to separate them from the rest of the text.

As the biography of each person is drawn, a picture of the whole set of ancestors emerges, and a number of stories are told. Finding echoes in the past of later events, or spotting certain characteristics running through the family tree, all adds interest to the tale. Then you can link the story up into one narrative, broken into sections but forming a chain of events up to the present day.

It is a good idea to tie family events in where possible with occurrences of national or international importance. This puts the whole story into a historical context. For example, the national story of the day or week of birth of a child can help to set the tone for that time. Developments in the area inhabited can also provide interesting background.

You can also make reasonable assumptions from the

circumstances of the time. For instance, if Thomas Muster's father died while his son was away fighting during World War I, we can assume he heard the news from a letter or telegram, and attended the funeral on compassionate leave. Another example would be if you have an ancestor who was a miner in 1842. That year it became illegal for women or boys under the age of ten to be employed in the mines. So before then, such people may well have been working alongside your past relative. Social histories of the period concerned will supply you with plenty of this kind of fascinating detail.

When it is appropriate, allow yourself to stray from the basic facts, and if you chance across some distant relative who proves to be of interest, don't be afraid to put that strand of the story in. That said, try to keep your stories concise, and imagine you are reading the story of some other family. What would interest you? Which facts are not needed to tell the tale, and clutter up the flow of the story? Leave each section you write for a few days then reread it.

Eventually you will have a document which traces the fortunes of your family across the generations and the centuries. As you find more or delve further into the past, you may want to make amendments or additions. Perhaps the most important additions as far as your current and future family is concerned is to keep a record of your own life. This should not be in the form of a daily diary, but rather a yearly summary of events, perhaps backed up by the photographs of key events.

You may wish to share your knowledge with, or ask for research help from, your local Family History Society. These have been growing rapidly for the last 20 years so there is quite likely to be one based near you. Such societies have regular meetings and often produce a journal including accounts of members' activities.

# SOME USEFUL ADDRESSES

Every care has been taken in the preparation of these addresses and telephone numbers, but some may change as time goes by. It is always advisable to phone or write (enclose a stamped self-addressed envelope) before travelling to view documents or indexes. An appointment may be necessary. Some organisations offer a postal copying service.

## REGISTRIES

The General Register Office
St Catherine's House
10 Kingsway
London WC2B 6JP
*Tel: 071 242 0262*

Scotland
New Register House
Edinburgh EH1 3YT
*Tel: 031 556 3952*

Eire
James Joyce House
8–11 Lombard Street East
Dublin 2
*Tel: 010 3531 711000*

Northern Ireland
Oxford House
49–55 Chichester Street
Belfast BT1 4HL
*Tel: 0232 235211*

Isle of Man
General Registry
Finch Road
Douglas
Isle of Man
*Tel: 0624 73358*

The Channel Islands
The Librarian
The Société Jersiaise
9 Pier Road
St. Helier
Jersey
(Postal enquiries only)

Principal Probate Registry
Somerset House
Strand
London WC2R 1LA
*Tel: 071 936 6000*

## PUBLIC RECORD OFFICES

Public Record Office
Chancery Lane
London WC2A 1LR
Tel: 071 876 3444

## SOME USEFUL ADDRESSES

Public Record Office
Ruskin Avenue
Kew
Richmond
Surrey TW9 4DU
*Tel: 071 876 3444*

Census Office
Land Registry Building
Portugal Street
London WC2A 3HP
*Tel: 071 405 3488*

Dublin Public Record Office
Four Courts
Dublin 7
Eire

Northern Ireland Public Record Office
66 Balmoral Avenue
Belfast

Northern Ireland
Registry of Deeds (Eire)
Henrietta Street
Dublin 1
Eire

## SOME OTHER USEFUL ADDRESSES

Air Historical Branch
Ministry of Defence (Air)
Room 411
Lacon House
Theobalds Road
London WC1X 8RY

The Anglo–Jewish Association
Woburn House
Upper Woburn Place
London WC1E 6BT

Baptist Union Library
4 Southampton Row
London WC1
*Tel: 071 405 9803*

British Museum
Great Russell Street
London WC1B 3DG
*Tel: 071 636 1544*

Borthwick Institute of Historical Research
St Anthony's Hall
York YO1 2PW
*Tel: 0904 43000*

British Newspaper Library
Colindale
London NW9 5HE
Tel: 071 636 1544

British Red Cross
Archives and Historical Exhibition
Guildford
Surrey
*Tel: 0483 898595*

Catholic Central Library
47 Francis Street
London SW1P 1DN

Central Reference Division
National Archives (GSH)
Washington DC 20408, USA

David & Charles Ltd (for maps)
Newton Abbot
Devon TQ12 4YG

English Catholic Ancestor
Hill House West
Crookham Village
Aldershot
Hants GU13 0SS
*Tel: 0252 621703*

## SOME USEFUL ADDRESSES

Crown Estate Commissioners
13–15 Carlton House Terrace
London SW1Y 5ES

Department of Social Security
Special Section A
Room 101B
Records Branch
Newcastle upon Tyne NE98 1YU

(Duchy of Cornwall records)
Estate Office
10 Buckingham Gate
London SW1E 6LA

Federation of Family History
Societies
2 Florence Road
Harrogate
North Yorkshire HG2 0LD

Alan Godfrey (maps)
57–58 Spoor Street
Dunston
Gateshead
Tyne and Wear NE11 9BD

Guildhall Library
Aldermanbury
London EC2P 2EJ
*Tel: 071 606 3030*

Huguenot Society of London
54 Knatchbull Road
London SE5

Huguenot Library
University Library
Gower Street
London WC1
*Tel: 071 387 4477*

Imperial War Museum Library
Lambeth Road
London SE1 6HZ

India Office Library
197 Blackfriars Road
London SE1 8NG
*Tel: 071 928 9531*

Jewish Museum
Woburn House
Upper Woburn Place
London WC1
*Tel: 071 387 3081*

London Topographical Society
(maps)
36 Old Deer Park Gardens
Richmond
Surrey TW9 2TL

Manx Museum
Crellins Hill
Douglas
Isle of Man
*Tel: 0624 75522*

Harry Margary (maps)
Lympne Castle
Kent CT21 4LQ

Maritime History Group
Memorial University of
Newfoundland
St Johns A1C 5S7
Newfoundland
Canada

Mid Glamorgan County Library
Coed Parc
Park Street
Bridgend CF31 4BA
*Tel: 0656 57451*

## SOME USEFUL ADDRESSES

Mormon Branch Library
LDS Chapel
401 Holywood Road
Belfast BT4 2GU
*Tel: 0232 659976*

Museum of Mining
Chatterley Whitfield Colliery
Tunstall
Stoke on Trent
Staffs
*Tel: 0782 813337*

Museum of Chartered Insurance
Institute
20 Aldermanbury
London EC2
*Tel: 071 606 3835*

National Library of Wales
Aberystwyth
Dyfed SY23 3BU
*Tel: 0970 3816*

National Library, Dublin (also
National Museum)
Kildare Street
Dublin 2
Eire

National Library of Scotland
George IV Bridge
Edinburgh EH1 1EW
*Tel: 031 226 4531*

Presbyterian Historical Society and
United Reform Church History
Society
86 Tavistock Place
London WC1
*Tel: 071 837 7661*

St Brides Printing Library
Bride Lane
London EC4Y 8EQ
*Tel: 071 353 4660*

Society of Friends Library
Friends House
Euston Road
London NW1
*Tel: 071 387 3601*

Society of Genealogists
14 Charterhouse Buildings
Goswell Road
London EC1M 7BA
*Tel: 071 251 8799*

The Surname Archive
108 Sea Lane
Ferring
Sussex BN12 5HB

Association of Genealogists and
Record Agents
1 Woodside Close
Caterham
Surrey CR3 6AU

Registrar General for Shipping and
Seamen
Llandaff
Cardiff
Glamorgan CF5 2YS

Tools and Trades History Society
Winson Grange
Debenham
Stowmarket
Suffolk IP14 6LE

# INDEX

Abbreviations
  names 77–8, 81
Apprenticeship books and records 66, 67
Army records 64–5
Australia, emigration to 74

Baptism certificates 33
Births 50
  birth certificates 10, 29, 32, 33, 35–6

Census Returns 10, 13, 38–41
  abbreviations 41
Civil records 10, 13, 33–41
Coats of arms 8, 12
Cousins 31

Deaths 51
  burial records 48
  death certificates 29, 32, 33, 37–8
  registration 33–4
Diaries 29
Document storage 21

Emigrants 73–5
Estate records 71–2

Family crests 12, 83–7
Family records 32
Family tree chart 17–19
  children 19
  lines of descent 19
  marriages 17, 19
First names 81–2

Gravestones 11, 23, 52–3

Heraldry 12, 83–7

Illegitimate children 33
  marriage certificates 36, 37
  parish records 45
Immigrants 12, 73, 75–6

Land records 11, 70–2
Latin words and numerals 20, 55
Letters of Administration 22, 61
Local History Societies 68

Manorial records 13, 72
Maps 68–70
Marriages 50, 51
  banns 47
  illegitimate children 36, 37
  marriage certificates 10, 29, 32, 33, 36–7
  marriage licences 47–8
  registration 33–4
Medals 29
Military records 13
Monarchs' reigns 44–5

Names 12
Naval records 65–6
Newspapers 12, 62–3
  obituaries 11, 29, 32, 63
  wedding reports 32, 63
Northern Ireland
  Census Returns 38
  civil records 33
  wills 60

Obituaries, newspaper 11, 29, 32, 63
Ordnance Survey maps 69

Parish records 11, 13, 42–55
  baptisms 45–6

## INDEX

burials 48
marriages 46–8
Original Parish Registers handbook 52
Photographs 29
Poor Law records 11, 54
Public Record Office 13, 38–41

Recording research 19–20
Relatives, interviewing 10, 13, 24–32
Roman numerals 20
Royal Air Force records 66

Scotland 11, 13, 33
Census Returns 38
marriages 47
Scottish Record Office 11, 13
wills 59, 60

Servants 40
Southern Ireland
Census Returns 38
civil records 33
wills 60
Surnames 77–80

Tenancy records 11, 70, 71
Tithe maps 69
Trade records 66–7

United States of America: emigration to 74

Wills 11, 13, 58–61
Workhouse records 54